YF-22 and YF-23

Advanced Tactical Fighters

Stealth, Speed and Agility for Air Superiority

Bill Sweetman

Motorbooks International
Publishers & Wholesalers ®

Pale Ebenezer thought it wrong to fight,
But Roaring Bill, who killed him, thought it right.

These lines by Hilaire Belloc come to me from my father,
a peaceful man who went to war.

First published in 1991 by Motorbooks International Publishers & Wholesalers, P O Box 2, 729 Prospect Avenue, Osceola, WI 54020 USA

Motorbooks International books are also available at discounts in bulk quantity for industrial or sales-promotional use. For details write to Special Sales Manager at the Publisher's address

Library of Congress Cataloging-in-Publication Data
Sweetman, Bill.
    YF-22 and YF-23 advanced tactical fighter / Bill Sweetman.
        p. cm.
    Includes index.
    ISBN 0-87938-505-7
    1. Fighter planes—United States.
2. Stealth aircraft—United States. I. Title.
UG1245.F5S965   1991
358.4'3—dc20   90-24883

On the front cover: Lockheed's YF–22 is the more conventional looking of the ATF designs, but Lockheed claims advanced features like thrust vectoring and its extra-large control surfaces give it the edge in agility. *YF–22 Photographic Team*

On the back cover: Northrop's YF–23 is the more futuristic ATF design. Its clean, sinuous lines give it the edge in speed and Stealth. *Northrop*

Printed and bound in the United States of America

Contents

Acknowledgments

Serious work on this book started in 1982, when I covered one of the first major industry/government meetings on ATF for *Defense Week* (thanks, Rick Barnard). I had no way of knowing that it would be the last such meeting to take place on an unclassified level. In the following year, I talked about new military engines with GE and Pratt & Whitney and at Wright-Patterson AFB, on behalf of *International Defense Review* (thanks, Charles Gilson). Once again, the vault doors closed behind me a few months later. Since then, with *Interavia*, *IDR* and *Jane's Defence Weekly*, I have covered the evolution of the Demonstration/Validation program and (when possible) interviewed many people involved.

Thanks are due to the many people who have helped with this book by sharing in their time, knowledge and experience over the past eight years. Al Piccirillo, Dick Borowski, Harry Hillaker, Ben Rich and Paul Martin are among many in the fighter-design community who helped more than they know. A word of thanks to Greg Field and the rest of the Motorbooks people.

And thanks for everything to Mary Pat, Martin and Evan.

Introduction

The fighter and the microchip

Most aerospace engineers of forty or over can tell you when they bought their first electronic calculator. Many of them spent $100 or more, in big, fat 1970 dollars, and bought themselves something that would add, subtract, multiply and divide up to four figures.

Even that was a competitive edge in design offices where access to the few computers, housed in their own rooms, was always at a premium. Some day, it might make a difference to the payslip which was pushed out every month with the aid of a punched-card reader, a device of Victorian ancestry. It might help win promotion to the plush upper floors of headquarters, where the subtle rank distinctions among executive secretaries were reflected in typewriters. The creme de la creme had IBM machines which could, with a few keystrokes, actually correct one character at a time.

Engineers with rich parents or doting spouses might even have been given a new calculator for Christmas, back in 1970. Three days earlier, McDonnell Douglas got one of the biggest Christmas presents in history: the contract to build the US Air Force's next fighter, the F-15.

It was a gift that kept on giving. The US Air Force took delivery of its first F-15 in November 1974 and, at the time of this writing, the F-15 Eagle is still the premier heavy fighter, and it is still in production.

One of the unsung stories of aerospace engineering is the longevity of its products. I read a book a few weeks ago about the U-2 affair of 1960. It was meticulously researched, but full of anecdotes about the spyplane's flimsiness. The author was no doubt elsewhere when, early in 1988, a thirty-two-year-old U-2 from the first production batch soared off a California runway and bagged a series of world altitude records before being sent to a well earned retirement.

A fighter has a tougher life, hammering through turbulence at high speed and low level, wrenching through breaks in air combat training, pulling sustained 9-g turns as long as the pilot can stand it. Despite increasing speeds and g-loadings, however, the life expectancy of a fighter has increased. The first F-15As will see their twentieth anniversary in service in 1994; had earlier fighters lasted as long, the Lockheed F-104 would have been one of the USAF's most advanced fighters in 1978, and the

USAF would have taken a large contingent of F-51 Mustangs to Vietnam.

Nonetheless, any aircraft has a retirement age; and when it begins to approach, the question is whether to replace it with a new aircraft of the same type (which was almost done with the U-2, and may happen to some C-130s), a modernized version of the same type or a new aircraft. The answer depends entirely on the new technology which has become available since the original aircraft was designed, because it is new technology which makes an aircraft perform a mission better, and better mission performance is the only justification for spending money on a new design.

At the start of the 1990s, four-function calculators are practically given away with breakfast cereal. Not only have computers proliferated throughout the engineering office, but in many places they have replaced the drawing board and the mock-up. This book is being written on a piece of equipment which out-guns what an entire design department might have relied on two decades ago.

The explosion in computer power and the implosion of the cost of that power has fundamentally affected every aspect of aircraft design. Technology based on computers or their use has permitted the design of aircraft which are faster and more maneuverable than the F-15, will be more reliable and will cost less to maintain and—in a technological leap which few if any of the F-15's designers would have believed possible—are far less detectable by radar.

In that light, the best way to replace aging F-15s is blindingly obvious. The F-15's replacement, in fact, has been under development since 1986, and under intensive study for four years more; it is the Advanced Tactical Fighter, or ATF.

Chapter 1

Top Gun 2000

**"If you don't own the sky, you can't conduct operations.
We've shown that a thousand times."**

—*Brigadier General James A. Fain, Advanced Tactical Fighter program director.*

"The fighter pilots should have an allotted area to cruise around in as it suits them, but when they see an opponent they must attack and shoot him down. Anything else is absurd." Manfred von Richthofen, Germany's Red Baron, wrote these words months before his death in the April 1918 offensive. They summarize a lesson learned in the first three years of air warfare. Since then, the lesson has often had to be learned again, more than once through defeat.

The lesson is this: air warfare has no fronts, no salients, no chokepoints and no fixed points of attack. Air combat units are mobile by nature and can direct fire against any target within their range. If a commander hamstrings his fighter squadrons with tactical restrictions, and his opponent is wise enough not to do the same, he places his units at a disadvantage. Richthofen was chafing at commanders who would assign his units to patrol a section of the front, to deter bombing and reconnaissance flights. A generation later, Adolf Galland smarted under Hermann Goering's orders to stick close to the Luftwaffe's bombers over England. Unable to

choose the time and place of combat with the Royal Air Force, Galland's pilots could not make the best use of their limited time over England.

The US Army Air Corps could study combat reports from Europe with some detachment and responded by changing its fighter plans. Until 1940, most of the fighters developed in the United States were designed to defend troops or fixed targets against bombers. Their range was short and their maximum operating altitudes were low. After 1940, the Lockheed P-38, originally developed as a fast-climbing interceptor, was modified as a long-range, high-altitude fighter; Republic abandoned its original, Spitfire-sized XP-47A and started work on the XP-47B, with twice the weight and power. Later, the powerful second-generation Rolls-Royce Merlin engine was mated to the North American P-51 to produce the best all-round fighter of the war.

The P-38, P-47 and Merlin-powered P-51 shared some attributes which distinguished them, as a group, from nearly all non-US fighters. In rate of climb and maneuverability (the classic fighter virtues), they yielded little if anything to their German opponents or to Britain's Spitfire or Tempest. They held a definite advantage in speed at high altitude. But they had vastly superior range. In the last two years of World War II, they roamed across much of Western Europe, either loosely escorting bombers— and the escort task was that of destroying the fighters which the bombers drew up—or conducting fighter-bomber sweeps, strafing ground targets when there were no fighters in the region. USAAF commanders could assemble large fighter formations over almost any target, while only those fighters which the Luftwaffe had based within the immediate target area could counter them.

In the jet age, the mantle of the P-51 passed to North American's F-86 Sabre. Bigger and more powerful than the contemporary Soviet Mikoyan MiG-15, the Sabre also offered greater range. Air

combat in Korea took place on the northern side of the thirty-eighth parallel, with the North Koreans on the defensive. The F-86 achieved a 4:1 kill-to-loss ratio and the North's ability to thwart air strikes against ground targets was minimal.

Even before the Korean War started, the newly formed US Air Force was steering fighter development in a different direction. Most of the research and development money spent on fighters in the 1950s went on aircraft intended to destroy strategic bombers or on tactical fighters which were, in fact, short-range nuclear bombers. Speed, range and electronic sophistication increased; maneuverability and pilot visibility got worse; and the new aircraft cost more to buy and to maintain.

Had the US Air Force gone into Vietnam, in 1965, with the fighters which it had developed in the 1950s, combat results would have been worse

The Advanced Tactical Fighter is intended to replace the McDonnell Douglas F-15 Eagle in the counter-air mission. This F-15 is in typical counter-air configuration, with four AIM-7 Sparrows, four AIM-9 Sidewinders *and a 600 US gallon drop tank on the center-line station. Take-off weight with this load is about 50,000 pounds, which became the target figure for the ATF.* McDonnell Douglas

than they were. Fortunately, the US Navy had, in 1954, ordered a supersonic attack aircraft from McDonnell; had changed its mission, in 1956, to interception; and had changed the requirements in many other ways. The designers at St. Louis rose above the confusion and created the F4H-1 (later, the F-4) Phantom II. The F-4 was to be used not only by the Navy, but also the Air Force and every other allied air force that could afford it. It was the only US Air

Like the F-4 before it, the F-16 set standards for a generation. In particular, its maneuverability and visibility have been emulated in subsequent fighters. General Dynamics

Force fighter to be consistently successful in air-to-air combat over Vietnam, even against technically obsolete MiG-17s.

Vietnam taught lessons, one of them old: US Air Force fighters had been most successful in combat when they were least restricted as to what targets they could engage and when. Another lesson was new: the first large-scale combats between supersonic fighters showed that battles invariably decayed from the engagement to their conclusion, with participants getting slower, lower and closer together. The latter stages of the battle were often decided by gunfire, not missiles.

Fast jet fighters also proved ineffective in supporting ground troops. Air Force pilots found themselves flying attack missions in the Navy-developed A-7, the A-37—a modified trainer—and the ancient A-1 Skyraider. The Army clamored for faster, more heavily armed, more expensive helicopters.

The fighter community's response was to develop technology and doctrine which would apply the lessons of Vietnam to both future limited wars and large non-nuclear conflicts against combined conventional forces.

Counter-air

The new doctrine was a re-affirmation of what had worked in Korea and Western Europe, and what had worked for von Richthofen. Originally called air superiority, it is often now called counter-air. Its primary goal has been defined as "the ability to achieve local air superiority at a time and place of our own choosing." Once this capability has been established, the commander can use it to clear the way for his airstrikes; to break up hostile attacks long before they reach their targets; and to hold hostile aircraft at risk of attack at all times, even in their own airspace.

The secondary goal of counter-air is to destroy as many of the enemy's front-line fighters as possible for the smallest possible number of losses. The definition of counter-air does not refer to regaining, or defending air control above the target of an enemy attack; it is assumed that the counter-air fighters will gain the initiative from the start, and will fight in concentrated groups when circumstances favor them.

Counter-air, as was proven in the 1960s, requires a superior fighter, one which outclasses its adversaries in every air-to-air combat regime. Close support for ground troops would be handled by a completely different kind of aircraft (such as the A-10 Thunderbolt II). The air-superiority fighter was known as FX. It would be as fast as an F-4, would carry an equally heavy armament and would have a better range, but it would be more agile, would offer better visibility and would use the next generation of electronics: a better radar and built-in electronic countermeasures (ECM) equipment. McDonnell Douglas's F-15A design won the FX contest just before Christmas of 1969.

US Air Force plans had changed greatly, under the pressure of technology and post-Vietnam budgets, by the time the F-15 became operational with the 1st Tactical Fighter Wing in 1976. In particular, the service had been persuaded to accept a smaller fighter, the F-16, as a replacement for many of its F-4s. The F-16 was defined as a "swing-force" fighter, committed to support the F-15s in the opening stages of a conflict, and to switch to strike missions once the hostile air attacks had been blunted. The F-15s (with the exception of the dual role E model) have been totally dedicated to counter-air.

Had war broken out in Europe in the early 1980s, this was the plan: F-15s based at Bitburg in Germany scramble and head east as soon as the E-3 AWACS aircraft detect Soviet aircraft leaving their bases and gaggling up into their attack groups. Directed by AWACS, the F-15s steer toward the incoming formations as the airborne controllers update the strength and course of the adversary. There is no problem with target identification; at this point, any aircraft to the East can be considered hostile. Up to 100 miles from their targets, the F-15 pilots drop their center-line fuel tanks, push their throttles through the augmentor gates and accelerate to near Mach 2, to give their medium-range AIM-7 Sparrow missiles the best possible launch conditions. Fifty miles out, they start firing their AIM-7s; little more than a minute later, they are embroiled in a high-g "furball," throwing their fighters through hard breaks and punishing scissors and yo-yo maneuvers, trying to get a shot with AIM-9 Sidewinders or cannon fire. As fuel and missiles begin to run short, the surviving F-15s break and use their last fuel reserves to light their afterburners and disengage.

The US Air Force has never had to use these tactics. The Israeli Defense Force-Air Force (IDF-AF), one of a few non-US F-15 users, followed this philosophy in air battles over Syria and Lebanon in 1981 and 1982. Israeli F-15s have destroyed almost sixty MiG-21s and MiG-23s, together with two Mach 3 MiG-25s without a single loss in air-to-air combat.

An important factor in the Israeli success was the relative performance of the F-15 and the MiG-23, the best fighter available to its Soviet-supplied allies until the mid-1980s. The F-15 is faster than the MiG-23, and accelerates faster; it is vastly more maneuverable than the MiG-23, which has a complex mechanical limiter to prevent it from departing from controlled flight at high angles of attack.

The F-15 pilot sits in his aircraft, under his huge bubble of laminated polycarbonate, like a cavalryman sits on his horse, with the sills of the cockpit below his shoulders and no part of his aircraft, except the vertical stabilizers and the headrest, above the sill level. The MiG-23 driver looks forward through a small, heavy-framed windshield and backward through a roof-mounted mirror, which is supported by another heavy frame in the middle of the upward field of view. To the rear and to the side, massive inlet ramps block what field of view is left.

What made the Soviet threat credible in Europe was strength of numbers. By 1976, Soviet factories were building more than 500 MiG-23s and MiG-27s (a ground-attack version of the basic design) each year, together with Sukhoi Su-17 and Su-20 strike fighters and improved developments of the combat-proven MiG-21. Output rose at a rate which shocked Western planners. By the late 1970s, the Soviet Union was building over 1,300 fighters a year.

In 1978, American reconnaissance satellites passing over Ramenskoye airfield, north of Moscow, discovered new fighters under test. They were assigned codes with a prefix indicating the site where they were first seen. RAM-J was a subsonic attack aircraft. RAM-L was a new agile fighter, about as big as the MiG-23. RAM-K was more of a surprise: it was bigger than the F-15, and much bigger than previous Soviet tactical fighters.

RAM-L led to the Mikoyan MiG-29, which entered limited service in 1983 and became fully operational in 1986. RAM-K was the Sukhoi T-10 prototype which, after a long and difficult devel-

opment, entered service in 1986 as the Su-27.

What concerned Western military leaders was the possibility—suggested by the previous pattern of Soviet deployments—that the RAM-L would enter service as a one-for-one replacement for the MiG-21, with the Su-27 replacing the MiG-23. The prospect was described by one analyst as "a high/low mix, with their 'low' equivalent to our 'high.'"

Surface-to-air missiles (SAMs) presented another threat to Western air power. The Soviet Union relies far more upon SAMs than the West, possibly because they can be operated by quickly trained conscripts, and it has developed many more SAM systems and built many more of them. The Soviet Union has mass-produced medium-range weapons such as the SA-6 and its improved follow-on, the SA-11. These missiles and their associated radars are mounted on tracked vehicles. They can keep up with armored formations, to provide protection whenever the formation stops. After an engagement, or after their radars have been used, they can be moved quickly across country before a strike can be aimed at the source of the radar signal.

SAMs are point-defense weapons, but by the late 1980s the Soviet Union and its allies had installed so many in Eastern Europe that they constituted a barrier. The barrier was not impenetrable; it could be damaged by defense-suppression aircraft, or overloaded by a large formation. Nobody pretended, however, that SAMs would not destroy many NATO aircraft in the first hours of a war.

In the late 1970s, tension and instability in the Middle East added another dimension to the problem. The F-15 was designed around European distances: but possible allied bases in the Middle

East were a great deal farther from the likely flashpoints. Many of the Air Force's tactical aircraft would need a great deal of help from tankers to perform any mission in a Middle Eastern conflict.

When the Air Force thinks about its long-term plans for fighters, trainers, bombers or airlifts (all of which are mission areas to which the service assigns several different types of aircraft) its first step is a "roadmap." The roadmap is a broad-brush strategic schedule, which can usually be summed up in one chart and covers fifteen or more years. It shows how the service plans to replace or renew all the different types of aircraft while avoiding peaks and valleys in research, development and production.

Looking at the fighter roadmap in the late 1970s, the Air Force leaders could see that both the F-16 and F-15 were young designs and could be further developed and improved. The most pressing need was for more long-range interdiction aircraft. In the early 1960s, the Air Force had planned to buy some 1,200 F-111s, but technical, management and political problems cut the production run to 500 aircraft, few of which would be less than twenty years old by 1990. Several studies, including ETF (Enhanced Tactical Fighter) and ATAWSS (Advanced Tactical All-Weather Strike System) were conducted to define what the next-generation aircraft might look like.

The fast, heavily armed and remarkably maneuverable MiG-29 is less refined than *the F-15 or F-16, but can certainly engage either on near-equal terms.* Bill Sweetman

11

RFI

These were little more than paper studies in the years of the Carter Administration, but in 1980 President Ronald Reagan was elected on a strong-defense platform. In June 1981, when the Air Force issued a request for information (RFI) on what was called, for the first time, the Advanced Tactical Fighter (ATF), it could be taken much more seriously.

RFI does not offer any money or any production contracts, and has unofficially been described by an Air Force officer as "a way of getting industry to pay for our studies." It does not call for any detailed design work, nor does it contain rigid specifications. It broadly defines a mission, the threat and a desired service-entry date, and seeks opinions on what features are feasible

Northrop's first ATF studies concentrated on lightweight fighters. Around the same time, Northrop and Germany's Dornier collaborated on the ND-102 design study for a small fighter with vectored thrust for pitch control. Northrop

and desirable for a new system to perform that mission.

Industry responded to the RFI with concepts which ranged from a 25,000 pound fighter (smaller than the F-16) to a Mach 3, 120,000 pound "battle-cruiser." There was some common ground, summed up by a McDonnell Douglas paper that emphasized "STOL, Stealth and supercruise" as the most important attributes for a new fighter.

STOL, or short take-off and landing, was desired because airfields would be attacked by "runway-breaker" weapons delivered by aircraft or missiles. If the take-off and landing run could be made shorter, the task of repairing enough runway to permit operations would be easier.

Stealth, or low observables, was controversial in 1982. The RFI was issued in the same month that the first Lockheed F-117 Stealth strike fighter flew from Groom Lake, in Nevada. Stealth clearly had a great deal of potential, both against radar-guided SAMs and in radar-missile duels with hostile fighters. A Northrop paper, published in 1981, showed how a Stealth fighter could see its opponent first and fire first, even if the adversary had a more powerful radar and a longer-range missile. But very few people involved were cleared into the highly secret F-117 program, and Stealth was generally regarded as an exotic technology, inapplicable to a tactical fighter.

Supercruise, or the ability to exceed supersonic speed without using afterburners, had emerged from numerous studies as a desirable feature for the counter-air fighter. High speed and high altitude would give SAM defenses less time to react; put the fighter completely out of range of smaller SAMs; shrink the lethal envelope of medium-size SAMs, because they cover less area at high altitude; and place the fighter at altitudes where missiles are least maneuverable. Supercruise appeared to be practical and affordable, largely because of engine improvements.

To these operational requirements, the Air Force added some economic considerations. From the P-51 to the F-15, each new generation of fighter had cost more than the one before and had been bought in smaller numbers. Even if the rise in unit costs could not be reversed, it had to be capped or, at the very least, drastically slowed down. Norman Augustine, president of Martin-Marietta, had extrapolated the trend to 2054 and concluded that, in that year, the entire US defense budget would buy one tactical fighter. Augustine said the Navy and Air Force could use it on alternate days.

In October 1982, representatives from most of the fighter manufacturers and many equipment suppliers, together with planners and requirements specialists from the Air Force, met in Anaheim, California, for what was, remarkably, an unclassified session on the ATF. In the discussion, the outlines of today's ATF began to emerge: a supersonic-cruise aircraft, with a combat radius of 700 to 920 miles (a twenty to sixty percent increase over the F-15), and with reduced observables if possible. It would be able to take off and land on a 2,000 foot runway, and it would be easier to support than the F-15.

The Air Force concluded from the RFI responses that range and supersonic persistence set a lower boundary to the size and weight of the aircraft, and price set a top limit. The requirements balanced at a normal takeoff weight of about 80,000 pounds for an interdiction/strike aircraft, and 60,000 pounds for a counter-air fighter.

As the Air Force was concluding that a strike aircraft would be thirty percent bigger and proportionally more expensive than a pure fighter, both General Dynamics and McDonnell Douglas were telling the service that the F-16 and F-15 could be modified for strike missions, and had built and flown demonstrator prototypes to prove it. The Air Force redrew its "fighter roadmap." There would be no brand-new strike aircraft: a strike version of the F-15 or F-16 would be developed (McDonnell Douglas was to win the contest with the F-15E) and the F-111s would be modernized and kept in service well past 2000.

ATF would be a pure counter-air fighter, a direct replacement for the F-15, using the best available technology; it would not enter production until the early 1990s, after the strike-modified F-15s had been delivered. Some 750 aircraft would be required.

The counter-air and strike forces were also inter-related. The new generation of Soviet fighters would have look-down, shoot-down radar and missile systems which would threaten USAF and allied strike aircraft in their low-level operating regime. If the ATF could engage and destroy these fighters, the strike aircraft could still hit their targets and survive.

RFP

The decision to optimize the ATF for counter-air meant that the Air Force now had a reasonably good idea of the ATF's size and speed, and, consequently, knew how big its engines should be. The request for proposals (RFP) for the ATF engine, then known as the Joint Advanced Fighter Engine (JAFE), was issued in May 1983, and General Electric and Pratt & Whitney were awarded contracts in September of that year to build and test prototypes of their competing engine designs.

In 1983, an ATF system program office was formed by the Air Force's Aeronautical Systems Division at Wright-Patterson AFB. Headed by Col. Albert C. Piccirillo, the program office's task was to produce a specification which met all the users' essential requirements and as many of their desires as practical. The traps to avoid were requirements of marginal value and disproportionately high cost. Every pound of equipment added to the aircraft meant a five-pound increase in gross weight to meet the same performance requirements. "Early in this stage," Piccirillo said a few months later, "we found four or five significant drivers [these were specific requirements which added a great deal to the fighter's weight] and making just one of them cost us 10,000 pounds." In other cases, Piccirillo said, "backing off by half a percent was important."

Piccirillo had good reason to know about the perils of procurement. As a new qualified fighter pilot, one of his first assignments had been to pick up brand-new, unused Northrop F-89H Scorpions from Palmdale, California, where they had received the last of many modifications and upgrades, and ferry them directly to storage at Davis-Monthan AFB in Arizona. Development had taken so long that the fighters were already obsolete.

After four complete drafts, the Air Force reached a near-final requirement at the end of 1984. Since then, only one of its most important parameters has been substantially changed. The 1984 requirement called for ATF to have an operational radius of about 800 miles, enough to allow it to cover the entire Central Region of Europe from bases in central England. ATF would be able to cruise at Mach 1.4-1.5 throughout that segment of its mission that crossed hostile territory (up to 300 miles in and out)

and it would be able to maneuver at supersonic speed. It would be able to operate from less than 2,000 feet of runway. The target for normal take-off weight was 50,000 pounds, about the same as an F-15C with its centerline fuel tank and eight missiles.

For the first time in any major program, the Air Force set and published economic requirements as well as operational targets. The flyaway cost—the price of one fully equipped aircraft, averaged across the entire production run—was not to exceed $40 million in 1985 dollars. The price was more than the F-15, but by a much smaller margin than the price of the F-15 had exceeded that of the F-4.

The Air Force also wanted the total life-cycle cost (LCC) of the ATF to be comparable to that of the F-15. LCC includes the cost of the aircraft, the spares and fuel that it consumes during its service life, and the cost of all the manhours required to fly and maintain it. Since the ATF would cost more than the F-15, the other components of the LCC would have to be reduced, by making the aircraft more durable, more reliable and easier to fix. The effort would concentrate on the engines and the electronics, because they are the biggest consumers of spares and maintenance time.

Reliability and maintainability also dictate how many missions each aircraft can fly in a day. The Air Force's goals in the ATF program were factor-of-two improvements over the F-15: a doubled sortie rate, to more than eight missions in twenty-four hours; a halved turnaround time between missions; and the ability to fix seventy-five percent of problems inside four hours.

A formal RFP called for bids on the next stage in the ATF project in September 1985. The only substantial change was that the Pentagon had cut the target price to $35 million. Seven companies responded to the RFP.

General Dynamics and McDonnell Douglas appeared to have the inside track. Builders of the F-15 and F-16, they had amassed a great deal of knowledge about Air Force fighter aircraft, weapons and pilots. Grumman had built the F-14; its handicap was that it was a "Navy house," and had dealt relatively little with the Air Force fighter community. Rockwell, which had finished a strong second in the F-15 contest, was so heavily preoccupied with B-1 work that its ability to respond to the RFP was limited. Boeing seemed a total outsider, having never built a jet fighter or a manned supersonic aircraft.

Lockheed and Northrop had not actually built an air-to-air fighter for first-line US Air Force use since the 1950s. Lockheed had built the F-104 Starfighter, which was smaller and lighter than the Air Force's other 1950s fighters and had a short career in the US Air Force. It was adopted by Germany, Italy and the Netherlands, however, and Italy continued to produce and modify the type into the early 1980s. Lockheed had also built the experimental YF-12 heavy interceptor in 1963, pioneering lookdown, shoot-down radar and missile systems; but its 1972 proposal for an agile fighter based on the F-104, the Lancer, was unsuccessful.

Northrop's last first-line US Air Force fighter had been the big and very subsonic F-89 Scorpion. In the mid-1950s, the company became a heretic in the fighter world, designing at its own expense a very small supersonic fighter,

A Lockheed "advanced fighter" study from 1982 depicts a completely opposite line of thinking from the ND-102: a high-and-fast-flying battlecruiser with sophisticated avionics and weapons for precision attacks on both air and surface targets. Lockheed

the N-156. The Air Force adopted it as the T-38 trainer and, several years later, decided to supply the F-5A fighter version to allied nations under the Military Assistance Program. It was followed by the much improved F-5E Tiger II.

Northrop was also early to spot the revival of maneuverability and visibility. In 1965 through 1967, the company produced a series of designs which began with a scaled-up F-5 and ended with a radical new fighter called the P-530 Cobra. After trying to interest several European companies in a joint venture, Northrop won a contract to build a Cobra derivative for the Air Force as the YF-17. The YF-16 beat it in the massive "sale of the century" contest to provide a new fighter for the US Air Force and NATO.

The Northrop Cobra design was adopted by the US Navy, but the service insisted that the program be led by a traditional Navy supplier, resulting in the McDonnell Douglas/Northrop F/A-18. Once again, Northrop tried to find an export market for a land-based version of the F-18, convinced that it would be a world-beater, but the fact that the F/A-18 was fully funded and Pentagon-supported, and hence cheaper for an export customer, told against them.

Instead, Northrop took the radical step of developing what was basically a new export fighter with company funds; although it was at first called the F-5G, its resemblance to earlier F-5s was superficial and it was later redesignated F-20. Once again, the company found itself frustrated by changes in Pentagon policy. The F-20 had been designed after the Carter Administration imposed strict limits on F-16 sales, because the General Dynamics fighter was considered likely to spark local arms races. The Reagan Administration dropped

these limits, leaving the F-20 to compete directly with the in-production F-16. Two F-20s were flown, and both were lost in accidents before Northrop suspended the program. However, the F-20 had shown Northrop's ability to develop and build a fully equipped fighter within tight cost and schedule limitations.

Stealth

What proved to be the deciding factor was that Lockheed and Northrop each had an ace up their sleeve: Stealth, in which both had more experience than any of their rivals.

Stealth had begun to mature while the details of the ATF requirement were being worked out. Between 1981 and 1985, Lockheed's F-117A Stealth fighter completed its flight tests and became operational with the US Air Force; and Northrop completed most of an extensive risk-reduction program on the B-2 bomber, with a great deal of emphasis on its Stealth characteristics. These programs forced the pace in technologies which were critical to Stealth, including radar-absorbent materials, computer-aided design techniques and test facilities. By 1985, both Lockheed and Northrop reckoned that they knew how to design a Stealthy fighter that would fly just as well as a non-Stealthy aircraft and would cost about the same to buy and to operate, and the Air Force believed them.

New sensors and electronic technology could be combined with Stealth to change the nature of air combat. The pilot could acquire and identify targets, and pick the most important victims (such as the most capable fighters and the command and control aircraft) before his own aircraft had been detected. He could also fire missiles well outside the visual range, with a good chance that his radar emissions would still be undetected. The target would still have no idea that his chance of survival was down to about ten percent. Colonel Piccirillo compared the new fighter's use of Stealth to the emergence of the U-boat in World War I; the objective is "to kill without being seen, disengage and disappear," he said in late 1985. "The last thing you do is surface and use the deck gun. Close-in combat is something you try to avoid."

Fighter pilots are no more like the knights of romantic fiction than any soldier in history, the real peasant-whacking lance-jockeys of the Middle Ages included. The aerial duel, one pilot against another, is an unreliable ideal. The longer a one-versus-one engagement lasts, the greater the chance that a third party will cruise into the arena and casually dispatch one of the contenders with a single shot. "There's a big luck factor in a dogfight," observed Piccirillo. "Ninety percent of people who get shot down, and come back, never saw who shot them down."

No surprise, therefore, that the program office was delighted when the first briefings from Lockheed and Northrop showed that Stealth, supersonic cruise and maneuverability could be combined in one affordable aircraft. In January 1986, the service announced that the deadline for replies to the RFP would be extended to late April, so that the other competitors could carry out more work on Stealth technology.

There was one final change to the ATF requirement, although it came too late to influence the outcome of the contest or the shape of the designs. Early in 1986, Congress took note both of the ATF program and the Navy's plans to develop a new Advanced Tactical Aircraft (ATA) for the medium-attack mission, and a new idea was floated on Capitol Hill: perhaps the two projects should be combined, to save money.

This would have been an unmitigated catastrophe. The Navy had looked at such a multi-purpose aircraft, called VFMX, in the early 1980s, and had decided it was unaffordable; likewise, the Air Force's early studies had shown that an ATF designed for the strike mission would be a forty-ton porker.

To forestall any shotgun marriages on Capitol Hill, the Air Force and Navy agreed to combine their programs in a different way. The Air Force would consider the ATA as a replacement for the F–111, and the Navy would consider the ATF as a replacement for the F–14. The agreement was deliberately vague as to timing (neither the F–111 nor the F–14D was due for retirement until the late 1990s) and the extent of the modifications that might be required to either aircraft. However, it meant that the winner of the Air Force's ATF contest might get a contract to build another 500–plus fighters for the Navy.

Managing development

As well as defining the design of the ATF, the Air Force devoted a great deal of time to working out new ways to manage its development. Air Force leadership was eager to avoid the pitfalls into which some earlier programs had tumbled, at great expense.

When the first radar-equipped jet fighters, such as the F-86D Sabre, were developed, the Air Force and the manufacturers attempted to manage the task as it had always been managed; prototypes were built and tested, and if the aircraft was satisfactory, it was ordered into production and the necessary parts were ordered from subcontractors. The problem was that the F-86D was a system that would not work without complex, specially designed subsystems, such as the radar and fire control computer. As it happened, the radar was late and, at times, there were 100 or more F–86Ds parked outside the factory, waiting for radars.

The weapon system concept was born from this experience. A weapon system is defined as all the materiel needed to meet the operational requirement: not only the aircraft, but its engines, radar, all other onboard subsystems, and the specialized test, training and support equipment and facilities required to operate the aircraft in the field. For each weapon system, the Air Force's Aeronautical Systems Division at Wright-Patterson AFB in Ohio would form the equivalent of a corporation's subdivision to manage the project. This was originally known as a program management office, but by 1982 was called a system program office. The program office boss reports to the commander of ASD and is responsible for the development and production of the entire weapon system.

Concurrency and its perils

Most of the serious problems in weapons development have been related to, or exacerbated by, concurrency between development and production. The classic example was the F–111. There was no true prototype of the F–111, because the first aircraft was built on the production line. Early F–111s were overweight and had problems with the structure and the engines; but the program was moving and it would be very expensive to stop. Only the last 100 aircraft met most of the specifications, and the 500 aircraft delivered to the Air Force were of five distinct types.

The total concurrency on the F–111 program did not allow time for unexpected problems, and it rarely provided for alternative solutions if these prob-

lems proved serious. Also, the idea of concurrency, in which everything was supposed to be taken from the drawing board to production in the same four- or five-year period, did not reflect reality. Some subsystems, such as the radar and the engine, could take longer to mature than the airframe.

The simple answer is to eliminate concurrency by completing development of the entire weapon system—full-scale development (FSD)—before starting production. Like so many simple answers, it does not work. It is horrendously inefficient—in time *and* money—because aircraft will not be available in quantity until three or four years after the decision to start production. It provides no protection against problems which emerge only when the aircraft or weapon enters service. It threatens the exchange of information between designers and builders; there is no guarantee that the complete, tested design can be produced affordably or that no problems will occur when the design is adapted for production.

Concurrency can be reduced by starting production after FSD has been under way for some time. This can help if problems are discovered early in the FSD stage, because production can be deferred until the gremlins have been exorcised. Problems discovered after FSD are as troublesome as ever.

Other ways of protecting against unexpected problems are technology demonstration and risk reduction, which are really two names for the same activity. The objective is to test new technology as realistically as possible, quickly and inexpensively, and to reveal the extent of any unknown snags. This is usually called technology demonstration when its application is generic, and risk reduction when it is the run-up to an FSD program.

One lesson learned from earlier projects was the importance of keeping technology alive between major programs. From the late 1970s, the Air Force had funded work on airframe, engine and electronic technologies. Results of this work included the Advanced Fighter Technology Integration (AFTI) F–16, which had a digital fly-by-wire flight control system, canards and other modifications; the AFTI/F–111, with a mission-adaptive wing with flexible skins on the leading and trailing edges; and the Grumman X–29, with its swept-forward wing.

Two later prototype efforts were planned specifically to support the ATF program. Early in 1983, the Air Force called for proposals on a STOL demonstrator which would combine uncompromised speed and maneuvering performance with the ability to use 1,500 foot runways. McDonnell Douglas won the $118 million contract to build the F–15 STOL/Maneuver Technology Demonstrator (SMTD) in December 1984. Pratt & Whitney was to provide its engines and their vectoring, reversing nozzles.

The other ATF-related demonstrator, was never built; or, at least, we do not know that it was built. It was discussed in late 1982 as a "survivable, supersonic fighter demonstrator" and was later referred to as the "critical technologies demonstrator." Both these terms were euphemisms for Stealth. It is possible that the project was terminated, because it was overtaken by the ATF itself; it is also possible that it was carried forward as a black program in total secrecy.

Similar efforts pushed forward the state of the art in propulsion and avionics. Engine builders produced prototype engines which were never intended to fly, but which tested new-technology blades, disks and other components in a real environment. "Brassboard" models were used to evaluate new avionics concepts.

It was a given, from the early days of the ATF project, that the Air Force would not go directly from a paper design competition into a single-company FSD program, because the risks

Although Stealth considerations would rule out forward-swept wings for the ATF, the Grumman X–29 would yield valuable lessons in the design of unstable aircraft and unconventional flight control systems. Grumman

would not be worth the potential savings in time and money. The Air Force had done this only once since the F-15; that program, the T-46A trainer, was on the verge of collapse as the ATF requirement was being put together, even though its technical goals had been modest.

One question was whether to fly prototypes of two or more ATF designs. Prototypes had helped the Air Force make a clear, speedy choice between the YF-16 and YF-17 fighters in the mid-1970s, by demonstrating an unpredicted, curable but expensive flaw in the YF-17. Building a prototype does not eliminate concurrency. A prototype is hand-built, and resembles the production design accurately enough to replicate its aerodynamic characteristics. Its structure may be heavier and is not warranted to last for many flying hours (both steps save time and money) and its subsystems are usually borrowed from existing aircraft. What it does is provide a very reliable base for predictions of the production aircraft's drag (hence speed and acceleration), maneuverability and handling limits.

The ATF team, however, was initially against building prototype aircraft. It would be so expensive a process that the Air Force could afford to sponsor only two competitors; if more than two promising designs emerged from the competition, some good ideas might be eliminated from the program. Nobody denied that airframe prototypes were valuable; the question was whether their added value was worth their very high cost.

Many airframe-related issues could now be much more fully explored on the ground than had been the case in the 1970s, because of the development of some important new facilities. The wind tunnel remains the most basic tool of aerodynamic design, but it has been improved by new imaging techniques: a laser source, for example, can be used to illuminate a given "slice" of the airflow over the aircraft, giving a very clear picture of exactly what is happening at a certain point on the airframe. The wind tunnel data are also supported by computational fluid dynamics (CFD), which models the airflow around an object by predicting the movement of each molecule of air. The equations which make this possible have existed for many years, but the task was simply too complex for human calculators or early computers. In the 1980s, supercomputers in the gigaflop range (billions of floating-point operations per second) became available, and these can process complex CFD equations at reasonable speed.

Radar-cross-section (RCS) ranges, the facilities for measuring a design's radar reflectivity on the ground, were also getting better. In the early 1980s, Lockheed upgraded the Air Force's vast RATSCAT range at Holloman, AFB, New Mexico, to make it more sensitive and accurate and increase the speed at which it could acquire data. Indoor ranges, until the mid-1980s, could handle only small models, but from 1985 onward, the Harris Corporation used its expertise with high-precision antennas to develop practical indoor ranges which could map the reflectivity of model targets as large as a half-scale ATF.

Another factor in the decision not to build prototypes was that many of the most important challenges were not related to the airframe. The USAF wanted the contractors to do things that had never been done before, such as putting together a complete prototype of the avionics system and making it work with a pilot "in the loop," at least on a ground rig if not in an aircraft. The Air Force also wanted a complete mock-up with access panels and removable parts, to show that ground crews could work on it easily, even in full chemical-warfare gear.

Dem/Val

There were also less publicized reasons for not sponsoring prototype aircraft: the USAF had secretly tested supersonic Stealth aircraft and knew how it was done. "There are lots of programs, many of them in the black world, that have given us a high degree of confidence that we can do this," Colonel Piccirillo told a group of engineers in October 1985. The Air Force accordingly decided to develop ATF through Demonstration/Validation or Dem/Val, a competitive program which included all of the above elements and a great deal of wind-tunnel testing, but did not include flying prototypes. This was the program defined by the September 1985 RFP.

In May 1986, Secretary of the Air Force Edward C. Aldridge announced that the Air Force would order flying prototypes of two ATF designs. Three factors lay behind the change of plan. One of these was the report of the Packard Commission. Led by electronics pioneer and industrialist David Packard, the commission was convened in 1984 to review the Pentagon's procurement practices. Packard was strongly in favor of "fly-before-buy."

Another influence was that Lockheed and Northrop led the rest of the pack in the Air Force evaluation, helped by their Stealth technology. "We had two excellent proposals," was one comment at the time, "three good proposals, and two who just didn't quite get the idea." Cutting the field down to two was easier than it would have been if there had been three designs in a close group at the top.

The third factor, once again, was Stealth. The fact that prototypes would be flown before money was committed to FSD would let the engineers push the combination of Stealth, supercruise and maneuverability that much harder, developing unconventional configurations which might be too risky if they could not be tested at full scale.

Another consolidation of the ATF program came in the summer of 1986. First, General Dynamics, Lockheed and Boeing announced an agreement under which they would team up to develop the ATF if any of their proposals was selected; a couple of weeks later, McDonnell Douglas and Northrop announced a similar arrangement. For the USAF, this brought the three middle-ranking contenders (Boeing had placed remarkably well) into the Dem/Val program.

For the companies, teaming meant that they could not lose completely, and it also meant that they could share in its costs. There was never any illusion that the Air Force would pay for the entire Dem/Val program. This was an era of tough contracts, and the Pentagon was the only customer. If the contractors were lucky and careful, the funds that

Another important test program involved the McDonnell Douglas F-15 STOL/Maneuver Technology Demonstrator (SMTD), with canards and vectoring/reversing nozzles. USAF

the Air Force allocated to Dem/Val would cover about half the cost of the work described in the contract. The alternative was no chance at all at a $65 billion production program.

YF-22 and YF-23

The final decision was announced in October 1986. Air Force Secretary Aldridge chose Los Angeles as the place to announce a Californian victory: Lockheed and Northrop were to lead the Dem/Val stage of the ATF program. Lockheed's design was to be the YF-22, Northrop's the YF-23.

It was to be almost four years before either design was revealed in public, as a shroud of security and non-disclosure enveloped ATF. The Air Force's program office was dramatically enlarged to handle the full size of the program; when Lockheed's team held its first customer briefing after Dem/Val started, they had to use one of the Skunk Works' secure hangars because none of their conference rooms was big enough.

In charge of the project was Col. James A. Fain, a former B-52 and F-4 pilot with a fifteen-year background in flight testing and program management. (Fain was promoted to the rank of brigadier-general in 1989.) Fain imposed tight limits on what the contractors could say about their ATF work, and acceded to very few requests for interviews. Reports on the project's progress became fragmentary.

Dem/Val was planned as a four-year program, and it is formally divided into three sections; the Avionics Ground Prototype (AGP), the Systems Specifications Development (SSD) and the Prototype Air Vehicle (PAV). The AGP is a test of the entire suite of sensors, transmitters, processors and displays for ATF and, although they were not formally required to do so, both contractor teams

also proposed to fly their systems in an airborne laboratory.

SSD is an umbrella term for several parts of Dem/Val. It included large-scale and full-scale RCS tests; the development and test of new airframe materials; simulation exercises in which the ATF was "flown" against hostile fighters and missile systems; and the demonstration of maintenance techniques. Northrop test pilot Paul Metz has described it as "minimizing the unknowns and 'I forgots' that have driven FSD costs out of the roof in the past."

Under PAV, each team has built two prototypes (known as PAV-1 and PAV-2), one powered by General Electric engines and the other by Pratt & Whitney engines. The YF-22s' center fuselages were built by General Dynamics, the wings by Boeing and the forward fuselages by Lockheed's Advanced Developments Projects division (better known as the Skunk Works); the Skunk Works put the prototypes together. The YF-23s were assembled by McDonnell Douglas in St. Louis, because team leader Northrop was swamped with B-2 work.

The teams were given some freedom to choose the main technological thrusts of their PAV programs. In both cases, however, what was most important was to demonstrate that a Stealthy aircraft could cruise at supersonic speed; that a Stealthy aircraft could be an agile fighter; and that their designs could combine all three qualities and be Stealthy, fast and agile. Aerodynamics, handling and engine-airframe integration were the primary tasks.

Both teams built weapon bays into their PAVs, for tests of weapon-release concepts. It is also likely that they have made some use of advanced materials, to test them in a real-world environment. There are some apparent differences: Lockheed, for instance, has elected to test a short/rough-field landing gear on its aircraft, while Northrop's landing gear uses many parts from current-production aircraft. Otherwise, however, the PAVs are internally conventional and use a great many components from current aircraft.

The PAV test program was planned, from the start, to be quick. An FSD flight-test program tends to be slow, taking thousands of hours, because it is meticulous. The entire operating envelope is mapped in great detail, and standard tests are performed many times at slightly different speeds and altitudes. The PAV program, however, was aimed at a handful of points on the edge of the envelope, and was intended to encompass little more than 100 flying hours for each design.

The PAV segment is not a fly-off in the normal sense, and to consider it that way is to misunderstand Dem/Val in a subtle but fundamental manner. From the start, the Air Force planned to issue another RFP to the competing teams as Dem/Val drew to a close, this time for the full-scale development of the complete ATF weapon system. The Air Force would assess the FSD proposals in the usual way, assigning point scores to each area of the proposal, before choosing one FSD team.

The final ATF decision is based on the data in the FSD proposal, not on the performance of the teams or the aircraft during Dem/Val. The role of Dem/Val, of which PAV is one part, is to support the projections on which the FSD proposals are based.

While the Dem/Val program and the construction of prototypes continued, the Air Force worked to refine requirements for the operational ATF. One major change took place early enough to affect the design of the proto-

types. Pratt & Whitney engineers, designing the flight-weight vectoring and reversing nozzle for the NF-15B STOL demonstrator, found that the problem of cooling the reverser panels (which took the full blast of the engine exhaust) was tougher than it had seemed on paper. The reversing nozzle began to look more complex and heavier by the month.

The final NF-15B nozzle included more than five miles of welds and included four-inch-diameter cooling pipes, while it seemed that the production nozzle would add 1,000 to 1,500 pounds to the empty weight of the aircraft. Late in 1987, the Air Force relaxed its STOL requirements and dropped the thrust reverser, to general sighs of relief. It was a perfect demonstration of the advantages of technology demonstration. Even if the entire NF-15B/SMTD program was to accomplish nothing else—which is not the case—$118 million would have been a small fraction of the cost of discovering the same problem in FSD.

Armament details for the FSD aircraft were also worked out while Dem/Val was under way. At one point, the Air Force's ATF program office let it be known that it was considering whether the new fighter should have a gun, or whether the effectiveness of new AAMs was such that the gun was no longer necessary. The howl of protest from the pilot community put an abrupt stop to that line of thinking, and—as far as present plans are concerned—the ATF will have a gun.

Missiles were a knottier problem. Supersonic cruise ruled out external weapon carriage. At least, the missiles would have to be carried close to the airframe, like the AIM-7s on the F-4 and F-15. Stealth, however, was hard to reconcile with anything except full internal carriage, with the missiles carried inside weapon bays. The problem was that none of the weapons in the inventory were designed to be carried internally, and their wings and fins would take up a great deal of space.

One solution would be to develop compressed carriage versions of the AIM-9 and AIM-120 missiles with folding fins. However, this would be an expensive way to go if the ATF were designed to carry these weapons exclusively. Also, developing reliable folding fins would be much more difficult and expensive if they had to withstand the aerodynamic stresses encountered when they were carried externally, perhaps on dozens of missions. But logisti-

cal problems could be nightmarish if the Air Force found itself with an inventory divided between internal-only and external-only missiles.

The final solution is classified, but it appears to be a compromise which allows for full internal carriage without constraining the ATF to specially designed or modified missiles. The price is a reduced weapons load (probably to a total of six missiles) when unmodified weapons are carried.

NATF

The Navy ATF (NATF) program has run about two years behind the basic Air Force effort. It became clear, very soon, that the two aircraft would be very dif-

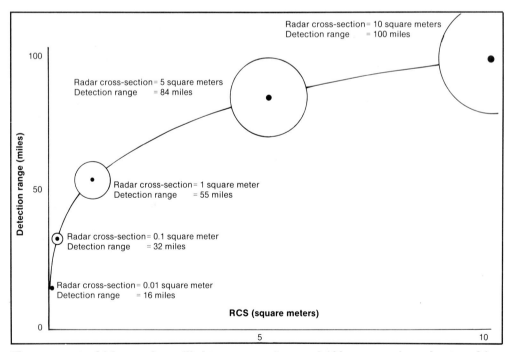

The range at which a radar will detect a target does not vary directly with the target's radar cross-section (RCS), but with its fourth root. Therefore, RCS must be reduced by a factor of 100 or more in order to achieve major reductions in detection range. Bill Sweetman

ferent, because the two aircraft have different missions—NATF is a multi-role fighter—and because the Navy ATF flies from carriers.

The Navy needs the NATF for combat air patrol (CAP), in which the fighters loiter hundreds of miles from the carrier to intercept bombers before they can launch their anti-ship missiles. The figure of merit is time-on-station, endurance at a distance from the carrier. The patrol line is to be reached efficiently rather than quickly, so supersonic cruise is not strictly necessary. Good CAP performance implies the ability to carry as much fuel as possible off the deck, whether internal or external. Stealth is not critical to the CAP mission, because the threat is to the carrier, not the fighter.

The secondary NATF mission is strike escort. In this case, it is more important for the NATF to match the range of the A-12, which has a combat radius of 900 to 1,000 miles, than it is to cruise at supersonic speed over hostile territory. The Navy ATF is also intended to carry heavier weapons than the Air Force ATF, for CAP and a secondary strike mission.

Basic carrier-suitability requirements are unbending. Not long ago, a Navy test crew showed a video of the F-14A Plus test program at a test pilots' convention. When the big fighter hit the runway at a vertical speed of twenty-six feet per second, a sort of muffled grunt could be heard in the auditorium. Land-based fighters are not designed to take that kind of impact (equivalent to pushing the machine out of a third-story window) and it is not efficient to design them that way because the weight penalties are large: Northrop once claimed that it could lighten the F-18 by 3,000 pounds if it developed a purely land-based version.

The Navy sets tougher standards than the Air Force for over-the-nose visibility, approach speed and low-speed responsiveness. The former requirement may mean a shorter nose and a higher canopy—both causing more drag, particularly at supersonic speeds—while the latter can mean larger flaps and slats, larger tail surfaces and a bigger wing for a given weight.

The Navy wants to fit two NATFs on one elevator, which measures 70 feet by 52 feet and can carry 130,000 pounds, because the ability to move aircraft quickly around the carrier is critical to launch and recovery rates, and hence to the carrier's ability to concentrate its airpower in the sky. Thus, the NATF, with its wings folded, can be no larger than the F-14 and no heavier than 65,000 pounds, fully loaded.

NATF will be heavier and possibly shorter than the ATF. It will have a bigger wing, a totally different landing gear and a stronger structure. The weapon carriage arrangements will be different. It will have better range and endurance than the ATF; it may not be as fast on military power.

In short, it will be surprising if the two aircraft have one significant structural part in common; the extent of the redesign is witnessed by the fact that the Navy is budgeting $8.5 billion for NATF research and development, almost two-thirds as much as the Air Force's R&D for the standard ATF. Lockheed's NATF design, for instance, has a new, longer-span wing and a largely redesigned fuselage. This has raised the question of whether the ATF and NATF must be based on the same PAV design and built by the same team; so far, however, the program office is adamant that the winner will take the entire program.

The USAF and USN plan to announce their choice in April 1991. The

ATF prototypes were originally planned to fly in early 1990. Full-scale development proposals would have been submitted in the late summer, and source selection would have followed at the end of 1990. Early in 1989, however, Lockheed indicated that its prototypes would be late. The delay stemmed from a June 1987 decision to change the YF-22 design substantially, in order to reduce its weight. The Air Force agreed to extend the program by approximately six months; in order to equalize its workload and keep its team together pending the source selection, Northrop also slowed its program down.

The YF-23 PAV-1, with Pratt & Whitney engines, was rolled out at Edwards AFB on June 22, 1990, and made its first flight on August 27. General Electric's engine, which powered the first YF-22, was flight-qualified later; the YF-22 was unveiled at Palmdale two days after the YF-23 flew, and made its maiden flight from Palmdale to Edwards on September 29. The PAV-2 prototypes took to the air in the following month, the second YF-23 flying on October 26 and the second YF-22 following four days later.

In early November, the first YF-22 became the first ATF prototype to surpass the Air Force's supercruise benchmark, reaching Mach 1.58 on military power after less than twelve hours in the air; although this represented a seventy percent increase in sustained speed for fighter aircraft, it was completely ignored by the mass media and largely overlooked by the aviation press. The YF-23 was not far behind, attaining Mach 1.43 on November 14.

Despite the importance of the avionics and systems demonstrations, the prototype evaluation has undoubtedly gathered more attention for the ATF than any part of the program. This is not surprising, because the YF-22 and YF-23 prototypes display the ambitious goals of the project in every line.

Frontal RCS figures in the 0.01 square meter range, typical of small birds and insects, were commonly regarded as fantasy in the early 1980s, but had in fact been achieved by Lockheed's extraordinary F-117. Lockheed

Chapter 2

Black Widow
and Lightning 2

**Follow the rules when you can, but when you can't, break them—but be damn
sure you're right. Above all, whatever you make must work!**

—Ed Heinemann, designer of the A–4 Skyhawk

Aircraft which are designed to meet the
same requirement can look very similar.
The classic case is that of the McDonnell
Douglas DC-10-10 and Lockheed L-1011
airliners, which were designed quite independently and ended up with wingspans
dentical to the inch. The YF-22 and
YF-23 are refreshingly different, in ways
which imply that the two design teams
have put a different cast on the US Air
Force's needs and desires.

The Air Force and other services
have learned over the years that they do
not and cannot know, at the requirement stage, exactly what a given capability costs to achieve. This is the kind of
detail which can only be defined by the
development process. Carving requirement numbers in stone before development starts can lead to the expenditure
of a great deal of effort and money to
meet a number which turns out to be
harder to attain than anyone thought.

A partial solution is to write the
requirement in terms of "required" and
"desired" values for each parameter. The
required mission radius, for instance,
may be 600 miles; the desired figure may
be 700 miles, and no extra points will be

awarded in the evaluation for exceeding
the desired figure. Applied across the
entire spectrum of aircraft performance
and characteristics—speed, acceleration, maneuver performance, payload,
radar cross-section and so on—this gives
the designer a great deal of freedom to
trade some characteristics against others. How these trades are made depends,
in turn, on the manufacturers' own
operational analysis and, more subtly,
on their assessment of what will appeal
most to the customer.

The ATF requirement was enough
to challenge any design team, however it
was read. It pulled the airframe design
in many directions, some of them dia-
metrically opposed to one or more of the
others. In some cases, two desired characteristics pointed to the same design
solution—which was then ruled out by
another, equally important requirement.
The intense conflict among all these
requirements is the root of the YF-22
and YF-23 designs.

Supersonic cruise, for example, is
not hard to achieve in itself. Given an
efficient configuration, with an arrow-
planform wing and a slender, carefully

area-ruled body, today's production engines could propel an aircraft at supersonic cruising speeds. With its sharp leading-edge sweepback, such an aircraft could be made Stealthy; but what it will not do well is maneuver, particularly at supersonic speed.

The designer can achieve long range with large external fuel tanks. The F-16 is an excellent example of how drop tanks can give a small aircraft a very respectable range. But neither Stealth nor supersonic cruising speed are compatible with large external stores. Another way to improve range is to make the aircraft bigger (the Sukhoi Su-27 has excellent range and is twenty percent larger than the F-15) but the Air Force had set a weight cap on the ATF, to keep the price down.

Stealth drives the design toward simplicity of line. The best way to reduce the RCS contribution of a component or a feature is to eliminate it: hence the tailless, finless shapes of the B-2 and A-12. Neither of these aircraft, however, need be agile, and both are subsonic. Supersonic aircraft have to be longer and slimmer and their wings are too thin to hold large fuel tanks or weapons. An agile aircraft needs a tail of some kind, and a body to hang it on.

It is therefore hard to pick out one feature of the ATF requirement and identify it as the crux of the design job. It was meeting all the requirements in one airframe which made the conceptual design process as agonizing as it was. The Northrop and Lockheed designers resolved some of these design conflicts in the same ways, so there are features in which the two ATF designs resemble one another, and, at the same time, differ from other fighter designs.

The first YF-22 is unveiled at Palmdale in August 1990. The sharp-edged hard chine that runs from the tip of the YF-22 nose to the inlets generates a strong vortex at high angles of attack which stabilizes the airflow and enhances lift over the body. The vertical tails are angled outward to minimize their RCS. Lockheed

In head-on view, the YF-22's angled shape recalls the F-117A, but inverted with the *wing above rather than below the body.* Lockheed

The most basic common feature is that the aircraft are about the same size. Since they were designed to have the same payload and range, and to use the same engines, this is hardly surprising. The ATFs are roughly the same size as the F-15C. The main difference is that their blended wing/body configurations have more usable volume, holding weapon bays and about sixty percent more fuel.

Another common, distinguishing and, like the weight, pre-determined feature of the two aircraft is sheer, outright brute power: power which is, above all, required to sustain supersonic speeds without the use of the augmentor (afterburner).

Engine thrust and weight

Each new generation of fighters takes advantage of a new generation of engines. In a fighter engine, the most important number is thrust/weight ratio. The best engines of the 1960s had a thrust/weight ratio of 5:1 (five pounds of thrust for every pound of weight). The F-15's engine, the F100, pushed that figure to almost 8:1, allowing the fighters of

the 1970s to set a new standard for acceleration and maneuverability.

When the Air Force was ready to write the specification for the ATF engine, the state of the art promised a thrust/weight ratio of about 10:1. The Air Force had a choice of two ways to take advantage of this improvement. It could keep the fighter's thrust/weight ratio (that is, the ratio of thrust to aircraft weight) roughly constant, producing a lighter and more efficient aircraft. The alternative was to keep the engine weight, relative to the aircraft, the same as it was on the F-15, and to take advantage of new technology in the form of greater thrust.

The Air Force did the latter when it wrote the specification for the ATF engine. Moreover, the new fighter engine would be more powerful in ways which the standard performance figures tend to ignore.

Engine thrust is usually quoted at sea-level and zero speed, and the figure which is used most often is maximum thrust with afterburner. The ATF engines have a sea-level, static, afterburn-

The YF-22 is shorter than the YF-23 and about as long as an F-15. The side-view is dominated by the vertical tails. Lockheed

ing thrust around 35,000 pounds, which is about twenty percent more than the latest versions of the F110 and F100. However, the new engine derives a smaller proportion of its power from the afterburner. Full military sea-level, static thrust (maximum power without afterburner) is at least thirty-three percent better than the newest F110 and F100, and fifty-seven percent better than the older engines that are fitted to most F-15s. But that is still not the complete story. At high speed, the ATF engines hold their thrust much better than the F100 and F110, delivering up to twice as much military power at normal combat speeds and altitudes.

Even using static thrust as a benchmark, the ATF has about the same thrust/weight ratio at military power as an F-15C on full burner; its pilot enjoys between forty and fifty-eight percent more thrust/weight ratio at all times. It is also interesting to compare the ATF against the European Fighter Aircraft (EFA), a rough contemporary. Although the EFA's EJ200 engines have the same thrust/weight ratio as the ATF engines, the EFA designers used that technology to shave 800 pounds off their power-plant mass. On the ATF, the same technology adds 7,600 pounds of thrust, and the US fighter's thrust/weight ratio is twenty-five to thirty percent better.

The YF-22 wing is almost a delta. The body above the inlets, aided by vortices shed from the nose chines, contributes significantly to the lift. Note how far forward the exhaust nozzles are located; this is because the new engines are short in relation to their thrust. Lockheed

Unprecedented military power at high speed is the key to supersonic cruise. It also helps to give ATF its long range. Because afterburners use fuel so fast, the total fuel required to perform the mission is strongly influenced by how much time is spent in afterburner. The ATF is designed so that its maximum speed, altitude and maneuvering performance are not much higher than its performance on military power. The afterburners are mainly required for supersonic maneuver, climb and acceleration. And the augmented thrust/weight ratio is so high that the aircraft accelerates very quickly, so maximum power is needed for little more than tens of seconds.

Aerodynamics

While the ATF engines could propel an F-15 or F-16 at supersonic speed on military power, aerodynamics are the key to efficiency, range and maneuver performance. Again, this gives the YF-22 and YF-23 some points in common. Although they are about the same size as the F-15, and have about the same span, both have substantially more wing area. Wingspan helps to determine the maximum lift of the wing, and an F-15-size span was necessary to meet maneuver requirements. The area is greater because the chord is greater; this makes it possible to have a lower ratio of thickness to chord (important in reducing drag at supersonic speed) while retaining the thickness, strength and stiffness needed for 9-g maneuvering.

For the same reason, the YF-22's and YF-23's wings are much more sharply tapered than those of earlier fighters. This concentrates area, and hence lift, on the inboard part of the wing and reduces the bending loads on the structure. Taper can also make the outer wing stiffer.

Prominent in this view of the first YF-22 are the large flaps, cut away at their roots to accommodate the stabilizer, and the very large fins. The flap area is enormous. Lockheed

Highly tapered wings are not ideally efficient. A wing works best when the lift is distributed along the span in a smooth elliptical curve, diminishing at a gradually increasing rate from the root to the tip. The YF-22's and YF-23's designers, however, could afford to take a trade in this area, because of the amount of power available.

Like the F-16's and F-18's, but unlike the F-15's, the YF-22's and YF-23's wings carry automatic lift-increasing flaps on both the leading and trailing edges. On both ATF aircraft, the trailing-edge flaps are in two segments on each side. The outer surfaces are flaperons, which work both symmetrically, as flaps, and differentially, as ailerons. It would not be surprising if the flaperons deflected upward at high-g to reduce the bending strain on the thin outer wings. It is notable that both designs include ailerons located well outboard, where they can be most effective. In some modern fighters, designers have accepted inboard ailerons to reduce twisting loads on the wing, but the YF-22's and YF-23's wings are clearly

designed to provide enough stiffness for good ailerons.

The F-15 and F-16 had set maneuverability standards for future fighters in terms of sustained-g at a given altitude and speed; it turned out that these standards were close to the limits of human tolerance. The ATF is designed to be a 9-g fighter, like the F-16. Maneuverability requirements set a minimum span and area for the wing, because all the technology in the world will not make the wing produce lift beyond its aerodynamic limits. Maneuverability also meant that the control surfaces would have to be big enough and far enough from the aerodynamic center to generate the necessary control forces; again, technology cannot create control authority that does not exist. Both ATFs have large and powerful control surfaces.

Another, less obvious common feature of the two designs is that the sides of the nose have a hard break or "chine" in front view, which starts at the tip of the nose and extends all the way back to

YF-22 pilot Dave Ferguson enjoys a near-perfect view through the totally frameless canopy, the first on a modern fighter. The nose and inlets slope away from the canopy sills. The canopy is treated with a metallic film of indium-tin oxide (ITO) to keep radar signals out of the cockpit. The canopy is reflective, but is shaped so that radar signals will mostly scatter off into space. Lockheed

the wing root. Other fighters have leading-edge root extensions or chines, but they blend smoothly into the fuselage well aft of the nose. The hard-chine forebody shapes on the YF–22 and YF–23 shed strong vortices at high angles of attack. The high-velocity air in the vortices stabilizes the airflow over the wings and, because the vortices are low-pressure zones, creates additional lift.

Vortices can also cause problems. They can cause unexpected buffeting around the vertical tail, or blanket it in low-pressure air and make the aircraft unstable. Asymmetrical vortices can cause sudden yawing moments when they are least wanted, at low speeds and high angles of attack. However, computer fluid dynamics (CFD) has greatly improved the understanding of vortices, and has allowed the designers of the YF–22 and YF–23 to make much greater use of the vortices' potential at a reasonable level of risk.

FBW

Both teams could take advantage of mature fly-by-wire (FBW) or electronically signaled flight controls. The F–16 and F–18 had shown that FBW could make otherwise unstable aircraft fly safely and reliably, by making tiny control corrections much faster than a human pilot, or the traditional mechanically-signaled system of rods and bellcranks, could do. Then, the B–2 and F–117 had shown that FBW, coupled with very large and effective controls, could make an aircraft fly well, even though its unaugmented handling would be unstable in all three axes and, in the F–117's case, afflicted with all sorts of unpleasant cross-axis couples.

For the YF–22 and YF–23, FBW has been refined and integrated with the engine control and the fuel system. It has become part of the vehicle management system (VMS). This is not just a buzz-phrase. Computers are constantly monitoring the operation of the aircraft,

The YF–22 takes off for its first flight on September 29, 1990. The small ailerons and leading-edge flaps are dropped to aid the much bigger flaps at low speed. Note, in this view, the continuous sharp edge from the tip of the nose to the wingtip. Lockheed

so that the most efficient combination of engine thrust and aerodynamic trim is always used. On the YF–22, the VMS adjusts the fuel flow from different tanks to balance the aircraft for optimum cruise efficiency; the result is a small but significant increase in range.

Both ATF design teams broke with a recent fashion in fighter design. Most of the fighters designed in the 1980s, including the EFA, France's Dassault Rafale, Sweden's JAS 39 Gripen and the Israel Aircraft Industries Lavi, have canards, or foreplanes, with delta or near-delta wings. At a technical conference in late 1987, two engineers were trading views on the best place to put the canard, when a third engineer rose from his seat and remarked: "In the view of General Dynamics, the optimum location of a canard is on somebody else's airplane." Northrop and Lockheed designers came to the same conclusion.

The intuitive reaction to a canard is that it makes sense to have a control surface which pushes in the same direction that the pilot wants the aircraft to go, unlike an aft tail, which pushes the tail down when the pilot wants to make the aircraft go up. An aircraft needs stability as well as control, and from this viewpoint a fighter with a canard is as unstable as an arrow with the feathers at the front. Fortunately, fly-by-wire can take care of this problem, and FBW led directly to the adoption of the canard for the 1980s designs.

Canard advocates argue that a tail-first fighter can have a smaller, lighter wing and a short, clean tail. Operating in clean air, rather than lying in the wake of the wing, the canard retains its effectiveness up to extreme angles of attack.

The canard has disadvantages that center on size and location. The foreplanes of the canard fighters are all small in comparison with the stabilizers of a tail-aft fighter, because of the area rule: a large foreplane creates a big bump in the cross-section plot. Even if

One of the YF–22's most unusual features is the location of the horizontal stabilizer, right behind the wing. It is very apparent in this view of the second, Pratt & Whitney powered, YF–22 on its first flight. Lockheed

the foreplane is a long way ahead of the wing (in which case it tends to block part of the pilot's view) its control power is limited by its size. The size and power of a conventional tail is unlimited as long as the designer can tolerate its weight, and this can make the tail-aft fighter just as agile as the canard, if not more so.

The canard also has a nasty departure mode in which the main wing stalls before the foreplane. The aerodynamic center migrates forward, leaving the canard with insufficient leverage to push the nose back down: it is a deep stall, from which recovery is difficult. The FBW system can prevent this from happening, but only by using limiters. Invariably, these slow the airplane's pitch rate, and reduce its responsiveness, well below the deep-stall point.

It is difficult to build a Stealthy canard aircraft. Operationally, the frontal RCS of the ATF was the most important one, and it was desirable to keep the forebody as clean as possible. A canard would introduce hinge lines and acute internal angles.

Perhaps the final word on canards should be left to Ben Rich, director of Lockheed's Skunk Works: "Birds fly well, and I've never seen a bird yet with its tail in the front."

Another common feature of both ATF designs stems from the STOL requirement. STOL was new to the world of fighters. Getting a fighter to take off in a short distance is not difficult, because of its enormous power reserves. Short landing is much more difficult. With its big wing, the fighter tends to float on approach, and to be over-responsive to changes in pitch attitude. At the same time, its big engine has a great deal of rotational inertia and resists quick and precise thrust adjustments. Once on the ground, brakes may be ineffective on a wet or icy runway, and parachutes are unusable in crosswinds.

The thrust reversers demonstrated on the F-15B SMTD were intended to provide both rapid deceleration on the ground and very responsive thrust control. On approach, the reverser blocks the main exhaust, the engine runs continuously at full military power, and the throttle lever controls the cascades which vector the reverse-thrust stream, moving the jets forward or aft to maintain the desired speed. Thrust reversal was deleted in 1987.

Without the reversers, the ATF needed effective flaps, to reduce its landing speed. This militated against the canard, which because of its size has trouble overcoming the large nose-down pitching moment which trailing-edge flaps generate. Both ATF designs have quite large flaps.

Stealth

Stealth, or low observables, imposed its own peculiar disciplines, which underlie some common features of the two ATF designs. The basic principle of Stealth design is that radar reflections cannot be completely eliminated, but that the aircraft can be configured so that the reflections are weak, and much less likely to be picked up. Like all camouflage, Stealth involves reducing the amplitude and brightness of the target's observables to the point where the target can no longer be reliably tracked against the background of noise that is present in any spectrum.

Stealth begins with the elimination of obvious, blatant radar reflectors from the shape. The next step is to concentrate the reflections on the smallest possible number of alignments. This applies particularly to edges, such as the leading and trailing edges of the wings and tail surfaces. Other breaks in the surface, such as access panels and doors, are contoured to conform to one of these alignments. Edge management is very visible on both ATF designs.

Vertical surfaces are also to be avoided, because they have a strong radar signature when the radar illuminates the aircraft from about the same level, or a shallow angle above or below it, as happens when a radar illuminates an aircraft at long range. On the YF-22 and YF-23, any flat surfaces are angled about thirty degrees away from the vertical, shifting their most visible aspect on to an elevation or depression angle where illuminators are less likely to be found.

Combined with the need for supersonic cruise, Stealth pushed the designers toward carrying weapons internally. Weapon bays disappeared from nearly all combat aircraft in the 1950s, because studies consistently showed that an aircraft which carried its weapons externally was lighter and more efficient; the structure was lighter, because it did not have a large hole in the middle, and although the fighter with external weapons had more drag on the way into the target, it had much less drag on the way back.

Stealth was also a problem in inlet design. The conventional supersonic inlet (sharp-lipped, with hinged ramps and prominent bypass scoops) is one of the best anti-Stealth features of a conventional aircraft. However, neither of the Stealth inlets designed before 1985—the overwing S-ducts of the B-2 and the weird gridded inlets of the F-117A—were in the least suited to a supersonic, agile fighter.

Most discussion of Stealth starts with radar, because radar can provide an enemy with more information at a far greater range than any other sensor. However, it is a waste of time to reduce

the radar detection range beyond the point where the fighter will be tracked by other means. After radar, the most useful spectrum for detecting aircraft is the infra-red (IR) band.

Many IR sensors, particularly those used in most air-to-air heat-seeking missiles, are mid-wave IR devices which work in the middle of the IR band (3-5 microns). This is the natural IR frequency of the hot carbon dioxide in the target's exhaust plume. Others are long-wave IR (LWIR) devices (8-12 microns) which detect the heat caused by solar heating or air friction over the target's skin. LWIR detector materials are more sensitive, but the LWIR signature of an aircraft is much less intense than its exhaust plume. Infra-red search and track systems (IRSTS) for aircraft have been designed and built in both wavebands.

The primary IR Stealth measure on the ATF is the engine; because it uses its augmentors less than most aircraft, its

An advantage which Lockheed claims for the YF-22 is that the aircraft sits low to the ground, so that most maintenance can be performed without ladders or platforms. The big wheels and sturdy landing gear are designed for operations from rapidly repaired runways. Lockheed

MWIR signature is much weaker. Two-dimensional nozzles flatten out the exhaust plume, making it dissipate more quickly. There is rather less to be done about skin heating, although the use of special paints and the avoidance of glints from flat surfaces may reduce the reliable detection range of a long-wave IRSTS.

It cannot be overemphasised that two of the technologies which make the ATF possible—Stealth and fly-by-wire—are based on computers. The F-117 could not be designed without the computers which modeled the immensely complex scattering of radar reflections from its surface; the more aerodynamic designs of the YF-23 and YF-22 rely in the same way on supercomputers. FBW, of course, depends absolutely on the availability of fast, lightweight and reliable computers.

YF-22 design

Common requirements have created common design drivers for the ATF, leading to features which are similar. Different design cultures at Lockheed and Northrop, and different readings of the requirement, have led to features which are not so alike.

Lockheed's YF-22 is monolithic. Most of the aircraft's mass—engines and inlets, weapon bays, landing gear and most of the fuel capacity—is concentrated in a single box-like structure, some 38 feet long by 20 feet wide at its broadest point. Most of the front end of the box is formed by the air intakes; the trunks curve sharply inward to the engines, which are mounted close together. There are three weapon bays: one on each side, outboard of the inlet trunks, each with space for two short-range AAMs, and a longer, wider weapon bay on the centerline, with space for at least four AIM-120 missiles. Lockheed designers have pointed out that all three weap-

on bays are completely behind the inlets, reducing the danger of hot gas and propellant ingestion when the missiles are fired.

The short, tapered, chined nose houses the cockpit, radar and much of the avionics. The pilot's seat is upright, not reclined, and the one-piece bubble canopy sits in a frame with serrated edges. (It is not known how the canopy is made Stealthy, but it may simply be coated with a radar-reflective material; because of its shape and position, it is unlikely to scatter radiation toward any hostile radars.) The aircraft sits low, and the main avionics bays, located on either side of the cockpit, are accessible without platforms or steps.

In head-on view, the YF-22's cross-section resembles an inverted F-117; the design reflects a modified, improved version of the "faceting" technique developed for the F-117, the shape being dominated by flat surfaces. These surfaces reflect most of the incident radar energy along one axis, and are angled so that, at most likely illumination angles, the energy is deflected well away from the transmitter. What is new is that, since the F-117 was designed, the advent of the Cray supercomputer has made it possible to model the reflecting characteristics of curved surfaces. The facet breaks are not as many or as sharp as they are on the F-117, and curved surfaces are used for the upper half of the nose and body and for the wings and tail. The junctions between the ends of the flaps and the body, and the stabilizer roots, are chamfered in the same way as on the F-117.

The intakes are plain and have no variable geometry. The lips are carefully angled to minimize radar cross-section in the most important aspects. With the inboard lip well ahead of the outboard lip, the inlet is a "two-shock" design. At supersonic speed, the inner lip generates an oblique shockwave which compresses the air and slows it to just-supersonic velocity before it reaches the outer lip. A smaller "normal" shock forms at ninety degrees to the airstream on the outer lip, reducing the airflow to subsonic speed. A well designed two-shock inlet recovers as much as ninety-five percent of the energy lost in the shockwaves in the form of compression in the duct, which increases the power of the engine.

Sizing is important for a supersonic inlet which is not provided with a means to vary its throat area. The YF–22 is provided with means to dump excess air in some flight conditions and to provide additional air in others. There are spill doors immediately aft of the top lip, which dump excess air from the inlet at low transonic speeds and low power settings (when the engines need less air than the inlets swallow). Auxiliary doors above the fuselage provide the engines with extra air at low speeds and high power settings.

A slit between the inner inlet lip and the fuselage scoops off the boundary layer which forms on the side of the body, and the inner ramp is perforated for boundary-layer suction. The air is discharged through finely gridded outlets over the wing.

Lockheed's wing is a trapezoid in planform, almost resembling a clipped delta, with forty-eight degrees of leading-edge sweep. Thickness at the root is about 3.5 to 4 percent. The leading-edge flaps extend to the tips, and the trailing edge is fitted with large plain flaps inboard and smaller, tapered flaperons outboard. In order to concentrate radar reflections on a small possible number of alignments, the leading and trailing-edge angles are reflected in the horizontal stabilizer, the upper inlet lip and

some of the lines around the exhaust nozzle. Similar relationships can be seen between the fins, the inlets and access panels and openings all over the aircraft.

On the first flight of the F-117A, Lockheed test pilot Harold Farley discovered that the all-moving rudders were too small: they were enlarged by fifty percent for the production aircraft. Later, showing a photo of the YF-22, Farley said: "We didn't make that mis-

The zig-zag edges around the exhaust nozzles, the speedbrake (between the vertical tails) and other apertures all follow the same alignments as the wing and tail leading edges. Whatever radar energy may be reflected is therefore confined to a few aspects. The auxiliary inlet doors for low-speed, high-power conditions can be seen above the center section, on each side of the rotary air refueling receptacle. Lockheed

The first YF–22 takes on fuel from the Air Force Flight Test Center's KC–135E. Inflight refueling was one of the first objectives of the flight-test program, allowing subsequent flights to be longer and more productive. Lockheed

Much of the YF–22's body is occupied by the very large weapon bays: AIM–9 bays to the side, and space for the longer AIM–120s underneath. Lockheed

take again." Indeed not. The YF-22's verticals are seventy percent larger than the F-15's; they are not all-moving but are fitted with very large conventional rudders. (The twin tails have led to the design being dubbed Lightning 2, after Lockheed's twin-boom P-38 of World War II.)

The verticals are large because they are located very far forward, above the trailing edge of the wing and only just behind the aerodynamic center of the aircraft, giving them a short moment arm. But their combination of height, outward cant (twenty-eight degrees) and forward location should mean that the fins and the rudders (which continue right to the tip of the fins) remain in clean airflow even at extremely high angles of attack. There is a large speed-brake between the verticals.

The YF-22 has a horizontal stabilizer, and its location is unique: on the same plane as the wing, it is so close to it that the flap root is notched to accommodate its leading edge. The tail arm (the distance from the center of aerodynamic pressure to the center of pressure of the tail) is less than the wing chord.

Current fighters, almost without exception, have stabilizers which are separate from the wing in the vertical plane, and their tail arms are multiples of the root chord. According to conventional doctrine, the YF-22 tail has an extremely short arm and lies in the wake of the wing at supersonic speed, reducing its effectiveness.

But the YF-22 tail is not like other fighter tails, because it is not the only pitch-control device on board. The YF-22 is the first fighter designed from the outset to use vectored thrust as a means of control. In under one second, at any thrust setting, the exhaust nozzles can move from rest to twenty degrees up or down, and back again. Both the nozzle and the engine are under the command of the flight control computers, which select the extent and rate of the nozzle movement according to the pilot's control inputs and the engine thrust setting. Thrust vectoring is blended with the aerodynamic controls; one may assume that it is used both instantaneously, as a kick to start the aircraft moving, and for sustained maneuver.

Thrust vectoring

Pilots flying the Harrier vertical-take-off fighter have used vectoring in forward flight (VIFF) as a combat tactic for years, but the YF-22 system is quite different: the nozzles go up as well as down, they move much more quickly, they are aft of the center of gravity and they are fully integrated with the aerodynamic controls.

Even on the NF-15B STOL technology demonstrator, the vectoring nozzles can generate 6,000 lb of vertical force, and the YF-22's engines are fifty percent more powerful than the F100s on the NF-15B. This should be enough to start the fighter rotating around its pitch axis very quickly, to stop it precisely at a desired angle, and to rotate the nose down with equal speed.

Aerodynamic controls can be sized and located to provide ample control power at a certain speed point, but become steadily less responsive at low airspeeds. Vectored thrust, by contrast, provides control power which is proportional to engine thrust, and can be much more effective at low speed.

Vectored thrust can also be useful at supersonic speeds, where the aerodynamic center of the aircraft tends to migrate aft due to changing pressure patterns over the wing. As that happens, the aircraft becomes nose-heavy and harder to maneuver in pitch. Blended with the aerodynamic controls, vectored thrust can improve control response and make the aircraft more maneuverable.

Thrust vectoring can also be used to shorten the take-off run—paradoxically, by deflecting the thrust upward. The take-off speed of the modern fighter is determined not by lift but by the ability of the stabilizer to rotate the aircraft around its mainwheels. A quick upward blast of vectored thrust will do this very nicely; the nose comes up, the nozzles switch aft and the fighter is up, away and accelerating long before the nose can think of coming down again.

One of the reasons that the YF-22 has its engines close together is to ensure that an engine failure would not be catastrophic, even during a vectoring operation. After an engine failure, vec-

The YF-22 inlets do not have large movable panels. Boundary-layer airflow enters the slot between the body and the inlet, or is sucked in by the dark, porous patches on the inner ramp, and vents through the dark-colored grids above the body. Excess air at high speeds and low power settings spills out through the doors marked "no step." The small lip on the body side, by the top outer corner of the inlet, is a vortex-control device.
Tony Landis

toring is presumably locked out and the aircraft reverts to aerodynamic control with a limited flight envelope.

One of the arguments against thrust vectoring has been that it cannot be relied upon as a sole means of pitch control, because engines are not held to such rigid reliability standards as the aerodynamic controls. The aircraft's safe flight envelope is determined by the ability of the aerodynamic surfaces to control it. The opposing argument is that the quickness with which the aircraft can move around that flight envelope is as important as the size of the envelope itself.

YF-23 design

The Northrop YF-23 is, at first sight, longer and more slender than the Lockheed design. The actual difference in overall length is not great, but this is a case where first impressions are correct; the main load-bearing fuselage structure, measured from the stabilizer trunnions to the front of the cockpit, is about 7 feet or fifteen percent longer than the YF-22's. Long and sinister, the YF-23 has been nicknamed Black Widow in commemoration of Northrop's first fighter, the P-61 night fighter.

From the side, the YF-23's sinuous profile is reminiscent of the SR-71. The impression from other angles is of a mass divided among three long bodies: the long, high forebody and the two widely separated engine nacelles. The forebody contains the cockpit, the nose landing gear, the electronics and the missile bay, deep enough to accommodate four standard AIM-120 missiles, with fixed wings and fins. ("Looks like a bloody Lancaster in there," remarked one engineer.) On the proposed production version, the forebody is stretched by another 2.5 feet to accommodate two weapon bays in tandem; the front bay is shallower and holds two AIM-9s. There is a marked chine to the body, but leading-edge root extensions, which Northrop virtually invented, are absent.

The YF-23 uses the same Stealth philosophy as the B-2. The entire shape is made up of two continuous surfaces, top and bottom. The surfaces comprise compound curves of constantly changing radius, and they are seamless; there are no creases or sharp folds, and there are no flat areas which are not horizontal. The top and bottom surfaces meet on a line which forms the planform of the aircraft. Except for the wingtips and the forward fuselage, every line in the planform is parallel to one of the wing leading edges.

The engines are mounted above the wing plane. The YF-23 nacelles are larger than they would be on the production aircraft, because they are still sized to accommodate the thrust reversers, which were dropped after the design was frozen. The inlet ducts curve in two dimensions, upward and inward, to shield the compressor faces from radar. The inlets themselves are neatly integrated under the wing, with the leading edge forming the forward lip of a two-shock system. One advantage is

that the inlets are removed from the forward fuselage and its thick boundary layer, so that the drag and RCS penalties of a boundary-layer scoop can be eliminated. Instead, the thin boundary layer which forms on the wing ahead of the inlet is removed through a porous panel and vented above the wing. Spill doors are visible just behind the inlets, and an auxiliary inlet door is apparent just ahead of the engines; these serve the same purposes as the similar doors on the YF-22 fighter.

Northrop's wing is outlandish, with the leading edge sweptback forty degrees and the trailing edge sweptforward at the same angle, and the taper ratio and aspect ratio are both in the realm normally occupied by deltas. The wing has more area than that of the YF-22, if measured to the centerline in the traditional way, but the two are quite similar if the sizes are adjusted to reduce the effect of the YF-23's unusual planform. Like a delta, the YF-23 wing can be structurally deep, and there is a great deal of volume for fuel in the YF-23's wing box.

The flap system is similar to the YF-22's, with one-piece leading-edge

Sinuous is the only word to describe the YF-23 in side view. There are three distinct bodies, with the engines and forward fuselage blended into the wing. Northrop

flaps and two trailing-edge segments on each side, with a flap inboard and flaperon outboard. On the YF-23, the trailing edge surfaces serve as speedbrakes: the outer surfaces deflect upward and the inner surfaces deflect downward. The movements cancel each other in pitch and in the vertical plane and increase the net drag of the aircraft. Otherwise, no conventional speedbrake is visible. After touchdown, the outer surfaces deflect upward as ground spoilers.

The "seamless" Stealth design philosophy developed for the B-2 has been adopted for the YF-23; both aircraft have similarly curvaceous lines in front view. Northrop

V-tails

While the YF-22's vertical tails are big, the YF-23's control surfaces are even larger. The Northrop fighter's primary pitch and yaw control is provided by two all-moving surfaces canted fifty degrees from the vertical, each of which is about as large in area as an F-18's outer wing. They are big because they provide all stability and control in both pitch and yaw.

The YF-23 does not use vectored thrust. The exhaust nozzles are located well forward, between the tails, as they are on the YF-22, and are of the so-called single expansion ramp (SERN) type; there is one variable, external flap on top of the nozzle, the lower half of the final nozzle being formed by a curved, fixed ramp. Where the Lockheed fighter has empty air behind the nozzles, however, the YF-23 tapers smoothly down to a flat web-like tail with a jagged end. The engines exhaust through troughs lined with heat-resistant tiles, as they do on the B-2. The exhausts are very well shielded from IR missile attack from below.

The V-tail's Stealth advantages are clear. On the YF-23, there are no acute corners or angles between the wing and the body, or between any horizontal surface and the fins. Northrop is reticent about the aerodynamic merits of the V-tail layout, although test pilot Paul Metz has said that the company "would change nothing" if the requirement called for a supersonic, agile fighter and ignored Stealth.

V-tails have been tried on a number of aircraft, but only two have been produced in large numbers—the Fouga Magister light jet trainer and the Beech Bonanza—and neither is exactly a high-performance design. (The V-tail on the F-117 is not quite the same thing, being used for directional stability and control

The YF–23 engines are above the wing plane, and the inlets are below it; the inlet ducts curve upward and inward. Northrop

only.) Enthusiasts have argued that the V-tail saves weight and drag; detractors (backed up by some NASA research) have asserted that the area of the V-tail should equal the area of the normal horizontal and vertical tails for satisfactory stability and control. The YF–23's V-tails measure, in total, about two-thirds the area of the YF–22's four tail surfaces.

V-tails are also subject to adverse roll. When the V-tails move to steer the aircraft left, for example, they also generate a rolling force to the right, opposing the desired roll for a left turn. With V-tails as big as the YF–23's, located almost as far from the rolling axis as the ailerons, this could be a problem. One suspects, though, from the projected vertical area of the V-tails, that the YF–23 is designed to be neutral in directional stability and that only small yaw inputs will be needed.

When it comes to high-alpha handling, the airflow over the wing and the V-tails will be interesting, to say the least. Most discussion of the vertical and longitudinal location of the horizontal tail assumes that the tail is in one location. This is not the case on the YF–23,

where the tips of the horizontal tail are more than seven feet higher than the roots. The YF–23's remarkable wing shape must also be considered; the outboard part of the tail is much farther aft of the wing than the root. The theory may be that because of the spanwise variation in the wing/stabilizer relationship, the entire span of the tail is never blanketed at any one time, even at high alpha. Pitch stability—if not control—may also be helped by the basic shape of the aircraft, with its slender nose and extremely broad, flat tail.

Materials

There will also be some distinguishing details of the two designs that cannot be seen. Both are pushing the state of the art in terms of affordable, lightweight, strong, high-temperature materials which, in some cases, may be an advance over the graphite-epoxy (also called carbonfiber/epoxy) materials used on parts of the current generation of fighters, and which form much of the primary structure on the latest European combat aircraft. Some of these combine the high-tensile-strength carbon fibers with a different matrix (the

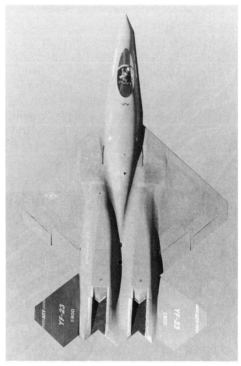

The rigorous approach to reducing the number of edges which is evident in the B-2 design was followed as closely as possible on the YF-23. The lines of the unique rhomboidal wing are followed in the massive V-tails. Also evident here are the heat-resistant insulating tiles which protect the structure around the exhaust troughs. Northrop

material which bonds the fibers together and gives the composite stiffness and compressive strength).

Boeing, for instance, has experimented extensively with thermoplastic matrix materials such as poly-ether-ether-ketone (PEEK). The epoxy matrices used today are thermosetting: once cured at high temperature and pressure in an autoclave, they are set forever. Thermoplastics can be remelted and reset, making them more forgiving in the manufacturing process because flaws

can be rectified after the part has been processed. For this reason, they may be attractive for large and complex parts where the likelihood of faults and the cost of junking a flawed component are both higher. In 1985, Boeing built a complete one-piece wing skin from carbon/thermoplastic composite, and this technology has now been used to build the wings of the YF-22.

Lockheed is also proposing to use metal-matrix composite (MMC) materials for parts of the production ATF, including the vertical tails. MMC combines the stiffness of titanium or aluminium with the tensile strength and crack-resistance of strong fibers. Carbon fibers are not suitable (carbon is too reactive); Lockheed has used MMC developed by Textron Specialty Materials, consisting of continuous silicon carbide (SiC) fibers in an aluminum matrix. Textron has supplied MMC I-beam spars, stringers and vertical tail skins to Lockheed.

This part of the ATF program is ushering in the era of "designer materials." With a wide range of fibers and matrix materials available, engineers will be able to achieve structural goals by fine-tuning the characteristics of the material such as density, tensile strength, stiffness and temperature resistance to achieve the best possible cost and performance ratio.

Radar-absorbent material (RAM) is very important to Stealth. RAM is based on the fact that some materials, such as certain carbon and ferrite compounds, absorb radio-frequency energy through a molecular resonance phenomenon. If a reflective surface is covered with these compounds in the right configuration, much of the radar energy which strikes it may be absorbed. RAM should be effective across a wide band of frequencies and at any angle. It should also be thin, lightweight, durable, easy to apply and cheap. Unfortunately, high absorber performance usually goes hand in hand with weight, bulk, inconvenience and high cost.

The F–117 was built using RAM technology which had advanced relatively slowly since the idea was invented in the 1940s. Since then, however, a tremendous amount of work has been devoted to RAM and radar absorbent structure (RAS) which is RAM that is integrated into the aircraft's skin. Better RAM was very important to the ATF designers. First, as noted earlier, an uncompromised low-RCS shape like

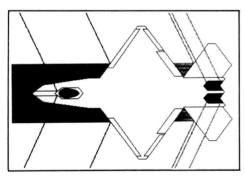

The edges of a Stealth aircraft's shape, and of all the access panels and major breaks in its surface, are grouped on a minimum number of alignments. Here, a radar signal transmitted from a point directly ahead of the aircraft is reflected along two bearings by all the reflecting edges on the aircraft. Neither bearing is close to the location of the transmitter. Bill Sweetman

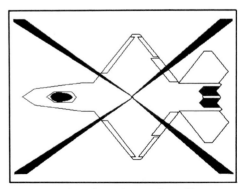

Grouping the edges along a few alignments also ensures that a radar will see the strongest edge reflections only if it is in one of four relatively narrow azimuth zones relative to the aircraft. The movement of the aircraft, however, means that the radar dwells in the sensitive azimuth zones for no more than a few seconds at a time. Bill Sweetman

that of the B-2 was impractical. Second, the addition of one extra pound of deadweight (such as RAM) to a fighter designed to perform at 9-g means the provision of nine more pounds of strength and lift. Third, the ATF adds a new dimension of stress to the RAM, because its skin will warm substantially in supersonic cruising flight. This may not only affect the structural properties of the RAM, but its electrical behavior as well.

Subsystems

Both ATF designs share other new technologies which may seem mundane but which nevertheless represent important advances over earlier aircraft. The ATF is likely to use a "smart" ejection seat with a computer controller which constantly senses the aircraft's speed, altitude and attitude and adjusts the ejection force accordingly. Such a seat is less likely to injure the pilot in a benign ejection (level flight at altitude, for instance), but can eject him much more quickly and forcefully, even at the risk of injury, if the aircraft is about to hit the ground.

The advent of the 9-g fighters led to the discovery of G-LOC (g-induced loss of consciousness). G-LOC is not the same as the familiar, gradual blackout phenomenon. It is caused by very rapid increases in g which outpace the body's responses; the blood pressure in the pilot's brain drops below a certain threshold, he becomes totally unconscious almost instantly, and does not recover immediately when g is reduced.

The YF-23's engine inlets are quite close behind the wing leading edge, so that the turbulent boundary layer next to the skin is quite weak and slots and scoops can be elim- *inated. The flat underside of the forebody aft of the cockpit indicates the location of the weapon bay. Northrop*

G-LOC has caused dozens of fatal accidents.

The ATF pilot will have an improved g-suit, which responds not only to the g-force, but to the rate of change in g, and which may squeeze the lower body over a wider area than today's suits. A system called Combat Edge, now being tested, will pump oxygen under pressure into the pilot's lungs, to raise the pressure in his thorax and slow the draining of blood from the brain.

Better g-suits expand the pilot's g-tolerance but do not help the pilot recover faster from G-LOC. To prevent a crash while the pilot recovers from G-

LOC, the ATF may have an automatic recovery system which will monitor the aircraft's speed and height above ground level, warn the pilot of a dangerous condition and—if the pilot does not react—pull the aircraft up into level flight.

Two other new subsystems are OBOGS and OBIGGS. These are not Irishmen but the onboard oxygen-generating system and the onboard inert-gas generating system, which produce pure oxygen and nitrogen from air bled from the engine. OBOGS eliminates the liquid-oxygen supply from the ATF logistics train; the nitrogen produced by

The YF-23's wing meets the body only a few feet aft of the canopy, eliminating the need for leading-edge root extensions. Downward view from the cockpit is outstanding. The hard chine from wing root to nose is prominent, as it is on the YF-22. The second, GE-powered, YF-23 is identified by an extra serrated panel ahead of the nozzles. This view shows the eight flight control surfaces: leading-edge flaps, trailing edge flaps and flaperons, and the V-tail. The outboard trailing-edge flaperons are almost twice as large as their equivalents on the YF-22, probably in order to combat adverse roll caused by the V-tails. Northrop

OBIGGS is pumped into the fuel tanks as fuel is used, making them less likely to explode if the ATF is hit. OBOGS also makes the aircraft less vulnerable, because it eliminates the fire hazard posed by the liquid-oxygen tank.

Reduced vulnerability

Reduced vulnerability is another largely hidden feature of the ATF. Most people, when they think of tough aircraft, think of armored machines like the A-10 and Sukhoi Su-25. But the discipline of of vulnerability analysis, which received a tremendous boost in emphasis after Vietnam, is applied in less obvious ways to other designs. Fuel tanks are located centrally, and positioned so that they do not drain into the engine bays if they are ruptured. Fuel and hydraulic lines are physically separated, and designed so that they shut themselves off if they are broken. One advantage of fly-by-wire is that it is immune from physical jamming. People who think that US weapons are somehow too delicate for the real world have never seen the photo of an Israeli F-15 which lost one entire wing in a mid-air collision with an A-4 and, incredibly, was landed, repaired and returned to service.

The long and careful development of the ATF requirement, and the Dem/Val process, have produced two aircraft which will outrun and outmaneuver any other fighter aircraft in the world. The basic indicators of fighter performance are wing loading and thrust/weight ratio; in these areas, both ATF contenders are between thirty and fifty percent better than the previous design generations.

Speed

The YF-22 and YF-23 are probably not the world's fastest fighters, on paper. The inlet shape tells us a great deal about the design Mach numbers of the two ATF designs. Fixed-geometry inlets can work efficiently at high speed, but do not retain their efficiency over as wide a speed range as a variable inlet. Both ATF inlets appear, from a rough measurement of ramp angles, to be optimized around the supercruise point of Mach 1.5 to 1.6.

The V-tails adopt a somewhat drastic angle to lift the YF-23's long nose off the deck at the lowest possible speed. Northrop

This is not to say that they do not work at higher speeds. The F-16, with its very simple inlet, can attain Mach 2.1 with two missiles on its wingtips. The ATF, with much more supersonic thrust and a clean configuration, should be faster.

The actual maximum Mach number is determined more by economics than technology. As an aircraft goes faster, friction between the air and the skin makes the airframe and engine hot. Aerodynamic heating increases geometrically with speed. At Mach 1.5, aerodynamic heating raises the skin temperature by 100 to 150 deg F, but the cold temperatures at cruising altitudes (-70 deg F) mean that the skin is no warmer than it is on the ramp in summer. But at Mach 2, the aerodynamic temperature rise on the skin is as high as 300 deg F; even in the cold upper air, the skin temperature is 230 deg F, which is as high as epoxy resins and conventional aluminum alloys can withstand in continuous use. At Mach 2.5 the temperature rise reaches 500 deg F, and an airframe which is not made from expensive high-temperature materials is limited to very short speed excursions.

In fact, striving for ultimate maximum speed in a fighter is probably a wasted effort. At its absolute maximum speed, where the drag is equal to the maximum augmented thrust, the aircraft has no excess power left to turn or accelerate and it is restricted in its means of deceleration, beyond a slow turn or power cutback. The F-15 can hit Mach 2.5 with a limited missile load (four conformally carried AIM-7s, but no AIM-9s) and a close-to-bingo fuel load, but one doubts that most F-15 pilots have seen 2.5 on their Machmeters.

The design maximum Mach number of the ATF is around 2.2 to 2.3. This is not quite as fast as the brochure numbers for some aircraft (Mach 2.5 for the F-15, Mach 2.35 for the Su-27), but the ATF is designed to attain its maximum speed with a full weapon load, which no other fighter comes close to doing.

Maneuverability

Fighter maneuverability performance has run into the limits set by

The trailing-edge flaps and flaperons work as speedbrakes on the ground and in the air: the flaperons deflect up and the trailing-edge flaps deflect down. The pitch and vertical moments cancel one another out, so the result should be a drag increment with no trim change. No other speedbrakes are visible. Northrop

human physiology, and ATF will probably not be able to pull more than the 9-g which the F-16 established as the benchmark for modern fighters. At subsonic speeds, the ATF's main advantage will be its ability to perform high-g maneuvers, climb and accelerate at the same time, breaking off from a combat without giving an opponent a chance at a parting shot.

Where ATF really expands the envelope is in the zone between Mach 0.9 and Mach 2. Current fighters need most of their augmented thrust to exceed Mach 1 and accelerate—at a diminishing rate—toward Mach 2. Their specific excess power (a measure of the thrust available for maneuver and acceleration) declines very rapidly above Mach 0.9. At Mach 1.5, however, ATF has fifty percent of its power in reserve.

ATF is believed to be designed to sustain a 6-g turn at Mach 1.8. Performance of this kind would allow ATFs to launch a first long-range missile attack on a hostile formation, sweep rapidly around the survivors without giving them an opportunity to engage, and then re-attack from the rear. If the ATF pilot detects a head-on air-to-air missile attack at long range, a 6-g supersonic turn-and-run maneuver will put the fighter out of the missile's range before it can close the gap. An ATF attacked by a SAM during supercruise can pull a 6-g break to evade the missile without slowing down.

These are basic design goals and, unless someone at Lockheed or Northrop has done their sums wrong, both designs will meet them. What accounts for most of the differences between the two, however, seems to center on the relatively new and hard-to-define concept of agility.

By the mid-1980s, fighter designers and operational analysts were looking beyond the conventional standards of maneuverability—measured in terms of g, Mach, altitude, and specific excess power—to qualities with names such as "agility" and "controllability."

No one has, so far, defined agility in a precise and universally accepted manner. It could be said, however, that agility is to maneuverability as "quick" is to "fast."

The main landing gear has levered suspension, with the wheels carried on trailing arms behind the struts. On the YF-23, the wheels are F/A-18 units and the nose landing gear is that of the F-15. Northrop

A fighter is considered maneuverable if it can sustain a 9-g turn at Mach 0.9, or if it can pull 6-g and still have power available for climb or acceleration; but these parameters do not tell you if the pilot has to "unload" to 2 g before he can roll the aircraft the other way, or how long that process takes. Agility can be defined as the ability to move from one steady-state maneuver to another; another definition, used by Northrop, is "the ability to rapidly change the direction and magnitude of the velocity vector"; a less official version, cited by Northrop's Paul Metz, is "the ability to shoot yourself in the derriere under perfect control."

Controllability

Controllability is still vague but slightly easier to define. FBW flight control systems have been described as carefree or departure free because they included computerized limiters that simply would not let the pilot leave the safe flight envelope. Some of these limiters are quite restrictive. If an aircraft's handling qualities become unsafe above twenty-five degrees alpha, for example, the limiter will not only prevent maneuvers over that limit but will increasingly inhibit the controls as that limit is approached, because a rapid pitch-up initiated at fifteen degrees could easily send the aircraft over the limit. Limiters also operate across different axes: for example, yaw and roll control may be inhibited at high alpha.

Controllability means that the departure-free envelope is bigger and that

The size of the flaps is evident in this view. Despite the elimination of thrust reversal, the YF-23 is still designed to require signifi- *cantly less runway than the 6,000 feet which the F-15 needs for normal sea-level operations.* Northrop

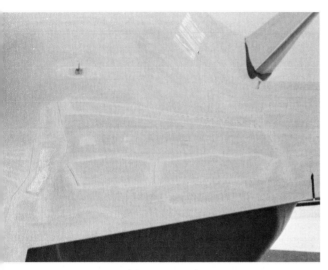

Inlet spill doors are visible as irregularly shaped panels above the YF–23 wing; an auxiliary inlet can be seen farther back. Boundary-layer air is vented through the porous skin panel to the left of the spill doors.
Tony Landis

The canopy is blended seamlessly into the skin shape, through unbroken compound curves. The head-up display is a Kaiser Electronics wide-angle unit from an F–15E.
Tony Landis

the pilot retains control of the aircraft in all axes over as much of the envelope as possible. The ultimate example of the agile, controllable aircraft is a purebred aerobatic airplane like a Pitts Special, which can turn through 180 degrees in bare seconds and which can be controlled in three axes at almost zero airspeed.

Such characteristics, however, were of limited practical use to the fighter pilot until the late 1970s. The main dogfighting weapons were the gun and the heat-seeking AAM. In order to use either, the pilot had to maneuver into his adversary's rear quarter, and fighter tactics evolved into a series of maneuvers aimed at turning an initial head-on confrontation into a rear-quarter chase.

Modern infra-red-guided AAMs such as the AIM–9L Sidewinder have made a critical difference, because they can be fired from any aspect with some probability of success. The lethal zone is no longer a cone trailing from the enemy's tail, but a cone extending forward from your own aircraft's nose. The ability to point the nose rapidly, predictably and positively in any direction becomes critical.

Rather more than Northrop, Lockheed seems to have designed an aircraft which can change direction quickly in a controlled manner. The YF–22 is shorter than the YF–23, so it has less inertia in pitch. It has an equal amount of horizontal stabilizer area, and it has vectored thrust. The unavoidable conclusion is that either Northrop has worked some black magic in an area not obvious to the naked eye, or the YF–22 will be capable of higher maneuver rates in pitch, particularly at low speeds.

Lockheed also believes that the YF–22 will have a larger limiter-free envelope than its rival. In many studies of V-tail designs, say Lockheed engineers, they never managed to make one that was departure-free beyond twenty-eight degrees alpha; partial or complete blanketing of the V-tail by the airflow off the wing caused a loss of pitch stability.

Many aircraft run into pitch limits not so much because their pitch stability is compromised, but because their vertical fins and rudders are blanketed by the slipstream of the wing at high alpha and they become unstable in yaw. The YF-22's tall vertical fins, and their large rudders, are clearly intended to remain effective and provide controllability in yaw at extreme attitudes.

Lockheed designers concede that their approach has not been free of penalty: the extra tail area adds weight and drag. The YF-23 is more slender than the YF-22, and it conforms more closely to the area rule, two important determinants of wave drag. The YF-23's rear end is a model of clean design, tapering gradually to a sharp edge; this could be most important, because boat-tail drag around the rear of the aircraft is notoriously hard to predict (the F-111, Tornado and several other aircraft have run into this problem) and can amount to forty percent of the total drag in some flight regimes. Other things being equal, the YF-23 is likely to accelerate faster through Mach 1, and it may also cruise faster. The differences may be significant. General Electric engineers have estimated that, since their F120 engine can propel the YF-22 at Mach 1.58, it could drive the YF-23 to Mach 1.8. It is probably no coincidence that Northrop, which lost what was then the biggest fighter contract in history to the F-16 on the grounds of excess transonic drag, has gone to such great pains to build a clean ATF.

Northrop's basic design also looks more Stealthy than the YF-22. It has fewer corners in its nose-on aspect and its inlets are more discreet. The edges are aligned on fewer vectors. Indeed, the YF-22 begins to look distinctly non-Stealthy from the side and rear, with the stabilizers, wing and verticals forming all kinds of corners and angles where the YF-23 has none. Lockheed designers do not deny some of these differences; their contention is that the rear-quarter and beam RCS differences are not exploitable; by the time an enemy can react, the YF-22 will be long gone.

Speed and ultimate low observables, or superior agility? It can be argued that your chances of killing the enemy and surviving are at their greatest if you move fast and remain unobserved as you launch four missiles at four targets. The idea is to hit the targets without getting involved in the visual-range engagement at all, because speed and observables count for less at such distances, and numbers—which are probably against you—count for more.

The counter to this argument is that, in seventy-five years of air combat, battles have nearly always degenerated in speed and energy until one participant is destroyed or both are forced to disengage; that the bolt-from-the-blue attack is an ideal but will not be achieved all the time in practice.

If these differences are real, and if the Black Widow and the Lightning 2 are as different as they seem, the question comes down to what the customer—the US Air Force—decides that it wants in a fighter aircraft. Either way, the Dem/Val effort has given the Air Force the largest and most solid database on which such a decision has ever been made.

Chapter 3

Thrust for supercruise

"All the good things in engine design come from high pressure ratio. So do all the bad things."

—A veteran engine designer

In 1983, the US Air Force did something right. It started development of a new engine for the ATF, even though it had not arrived at a final set of requirements for the aircraft. It was the right thing to do, for two reasons.

Engines have always taken longer to develop than airframes. Even the Rolls-Royce Merlin engines which powered the first production Hurricanes and Spitfires suffered from low power and reliability problems. In the 1950s, engine failures plagued many flight-test programs, causing severe delays; when the engine is unreliable, the testing of the airframe and every other element of the system proceeds at a snail's pace until it can be fixed.

The Air Force's most recent brush with this problem concerned the Pratt & Whitney F100 engine for the F-15. The F100, as noted in the previous chapter, offered a much higher thrust/weight ratio than the generation of engines before it, and was essential to the F-15's combination of speed and maneuverability. Full-scale development of the engine, however, did not start until February 1970, three months after McDonnell Douglas had been selected to build the aircraft.

The F100 did achieve its basic performance goals. To cut a long and painful story short, however, it was not until the early 1980s that the Air Force received F100s which were reliable, durable, easy to maintain and free of handling problems. One reason for starting the ATF engine so early was to deliver such a mature engine from the start of the program; there would be time to test the engines to breaking point and to fix any faults that the tests revealed.

The other reason for an early start was that the ATF engine would represent as big an advance over the previous generation as the F100 had done, mainly because of the Air Force's supersonic cruise requirement.

Afterburner

Today's fighters are subsonic aircraft which can sprint at supersonic speeds on augmented thrust. The augmentor, or afterburner, is a simple device: a set of flameholders in the exhaust stream that burn fuel with the oxygen remaining in the jet exhaust. This boosts the temperature and pressure of the gas stream, increasing both exhaust velocity and thrust.

The afterburner is inefficient. Compared with the basic engine, it uses much more fuel for every pound of thrust that it provides. Its advantage is that it is light. The F100's augmentor produces forty percent of the maximum thrust but accounts for less than twenty percent of the weight. A non-afterburning engine of the same thrust would have been 1,000 pounds heavier.

In the F100 and older engines, the afterburner was necessary if the aircraft was to achieve supersonic speed at all, because the engine's non-augmented or military power actually declined at high

speed. This is because the inlet of any jet engine decelerates the high-speed airflow entering the intake (although the air is really static and the airplane is moving, it is easier to think of the air as moving when discussing inlets) and compresses it, so that it can expand on the way out of the engine and generate thrust. When the air is compressed it gets hot. The pressure rise is magnified by the pressure ratio in the engine, so that the temperatures in the engine increase even more steeply with speed than the temperature in the inlet. In today's engines the turbine reaches its maximum design temperature at a speed of about Mach 1. At higher speeds, the flow of fuel into the engine combustor has to be reduced to hold the temperature constant. Above Mach 1,

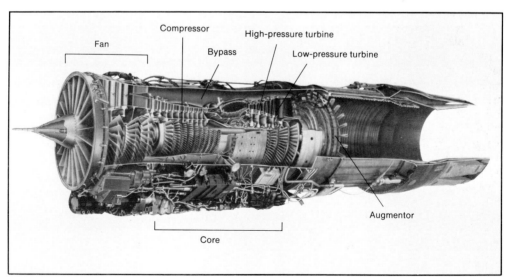

Cutaway view of a Pratt & Whitney F100 shows the main features of a modern fighter engine. From right to left, air passes through the fan and is split between the outer bypass duct and the core. The core flow is further compressed, heated in the combustor, and expands through the high-pressure and low- *pressure turbines. More than 40 percent of the maximum thrust is produced in the augmentor when fuel is burned in the mixed core and bypass streams. The ATF engines are similar in basic layout, but have fewer stages. Pratt & Whitney*

the only source of more thrust is the augmentor.

Supersonic-cruise aircraft such as the Concorde get around this problem with engines which have a lower pressure ratio, so that the temperatures in the engine can be kept within limits at high speed. The snag is that such engines produce less thrust at low speeds, in proportion to their weight, and are less efficient.

The ATF engines would simply have to run much hotter than the F100 and produce more thrust, without augmentor, at supersonic speeds. Tolerating higher temperatures is a matter of design and materials; developing more high-speed thrust involves changes to the engine cycle.

Bypass ratio

The F-111 engine, the TF30, was one of the first military turbofans. This engine had a medium bypass ratio, meaning that the airflow was split behind the first compressor stages (known as the fan), and roughly half the air was fed directly into the augmentor. The compressor, combustor and turbine (the core) could be kept small and efficient. On military power, at subsonic speeds, the engine was made more efficient by the larger, slower airflow. The turbofan fed a large cool stream into the augmentor, which could generate a great deal of extra thrust for a little weight. The next-generation engine, the F100, used the same cycle.

The ATF engine, however, needed a much higher military-power exhaust velocity to supply the needed supersonic thrust. This means reducing the bypass ratio until the engine is almost a turbojet, squeezing all the air through the core and expanding it to higher velocity at the nozzle. The core would be much larger, and it would be a challenge to keep its weight down.

The task of designing an engine with the necessary thrust/weight ratio for supersonic cruise was made even more challenging by requirements of Stealth and STOL. The primary means of reducing the infra-red signature of a jet aircraft, which is concentrated in its exhaust plume, is to flatten the plume through a two-dimensional nozzle. This increases the ratio of the plume's perimeter to its cross-section and causes it to dissipate much more quickly than the very stable round plume. But the ideal shape for any pressure vessel (such as the final nozzle of a jet engine) is round, and any variation in that shape means a weight increase. It was also clear that the kind of thrust-reversing nozzle that the Air Force wanted for STOL purposes would be heavy.

Achieving the necessary thrust/weight ratio in the ATF engine depended on advances in the two basic areas of engine technology: aerodynamics and structural design. Computers were essential in one area and extremely helpful in the other.

Engine aerodynamics

The impact of computational fluid dynamics (CFD) on airframe design has already been mentioned. However, CFD was even more important to engine aerodynamics, because the engine designer has no real equivalent of a wind tunnel; no one has yet designed and built a facility that will test a compressor or turbine blade under realistic conditions before it is built into an engine. Between the design of the F100 and the creation of the ATF engines, CFD made a very visible difference to engine design.

The key was the ability to run computer models of the airflow over a compressor or turbine blade in three dimensions, taking account of the end-wall effects—where the blade meets the rotor and the case—and of the changing velocity of the air from root to tip. Before this was done, designers had tended to be conservative in the degree of twist and spanwise variation which they designed into their blades, and had kept them relatively long and slender to reduce the importance of the uncharted end-wall effects.

With CFD, designers have been able to design thicker, shorter, more twisted blades which can do considerably more work, just as a thicker, more cambered wing will generate more lift than a thin flat wing. The advantages are many. There are fewer blades on each stage. The fatter blades attach to the disk over a wider area, so the disk-to-blade junction can be made stronger. Therefore, the disk can spin faster without the risk of a failure and, just like a high-revving car engine, can do more work. This, in turn, means that each row of blades, or stage, can generate a greater rise in pressure, and that the number of stages in the engine can be reduced. While it took the F100 ten compressor stages to achieve a 25:1 pressure ratio, a new engine can achieve the same ratio in five stages. The entire engine becomes shorter, lighter, stiffer and has fewer parts.

New blade designs are important in the turbine, as well. The entire turbine can be reduced to two stages, and the number of blades in each stage can be cut. This is important because gas temperatures in the turbine are well above the limits of any metal. The turbine blades stay in one piece only because each blade is provided with a labyrinth of air-cooling passages, some of them little thicker than a pin, which carry away heat from the metal and shed a film of relatively cool air over the surface of the blade. The ability to cool the blades is limited, however, because the cooling air has to be drawn from the

high-pressure compressor; pulling out too much air degrades the efficiency of the engine and actually makes it run hotter for a given thrust level, defeating the object of the exercise. If there are fewer turbine blades, the cooling air supply can be more concentrated, and the thicker new-technology blades can be designed with more efficient internal cooling.

The high-pressure turbine blades in the F100 were little larger than one's thumb. To drive the high-pressure compressor, each blade had to extract no less than 400 horsepower from the gas stream. The blades in the ATF engines must be in the 800 horsepower class.

New materials and processes have also been applied to the new engines. Some of them have been introduced into later versions of current engines such as the F100 and General Electric F404. Generally, however, the newer engines will use them to better effect, because the design can take advantage of the new materials from the outset.

Structural design

Where computers play a role in structural design is in predicting loads and stresses. Traditionally, engine components were designed to withstand the loads which the engineers predicted for a certain number of hours and flight cycles, after which the engine was removed and overhauled. The time between overhauls could be extended gradually during the engine's service career if close inspection of selected engines showed that they could last longer. Now, more subtle analysis of fracture mechanics (the forces needed to break a component, both when it is in perfect condition and when it has been damaged) has enabled engineers to demonstrate that a component will be safe from failure as long as no damage can be detected in routine inspections. The result is engines which will last as long as the aircraft remains in service: ATF engines are being tested to 4,000 flight cycles.

The complex modeling of fatigue and fracture mechanics was once confined to the compressor and turbine rotors and shafts, the most critical components of the engine. Now that computer power is relatively cheap and widely available, however, the same techniques are being applied to accessories: lines, actuators and valves.

New materials

The engines will use a range of new materials developed over the last twenty years. Some of these have been made possible by rapid solidification rate (RSR) metallurgy. Molten metal is dripped on to a rapidly spinning disk, which throws the material off in tiny

An early XF119 engine on a test run at West Palm Beach, Florida. Note the overlapping inner and outer panels of the vectoring nozzle. Cascades visible beneath the nozzle show that it incorporates thrust reversers, later discarded by the Air Force. Pratt & Whitney

droplets. These droplets are then cooled very rapidly in an inert gas such as argon, resulting in a very pure metal powder. The advantage of RSR is that different metals can be combined into pure alloys at a speed which outstrips secondary reactions between them, so that the metallurgist can create alloys which could not be made in a conventional furnace. RSR alloys can tolerate higher temperatures: RSR titanium can replace heavier nickel alloys, and RSR aluminum can replace more expensive titanium.

RSR powders can be formed directly into compressor disks by processes such as hot isostatic pressing (HIP), in which the powder is forged into shape at high pressure and temperature in an inert atmosphere. On the ATF engines, these techniques are being used to create "blisks," blades and disks formed in one piece, saving dozens of parts.

Composite materials are likely to be found in some parts of the ATF engine. Most temperatures around a military engine are too high for epoxies to withstand, but polyimide resins and metal-matrix composites (MMC) may be applicable. Current production versions of the General Electric F404 engine, for example, have a carbon fiber composite outer bypass duct made with a polyimide resin called PMR-15.

Features such as single-crystal turbine blades and full-authority digital engine control, gradually introduced on both military and commercial production engines over the past ten years, will be standard on the ATF engines.

Another lesson in risk reduction was learned from the 1970s and applied to the ATF program: competition spurs manufacturers to perform and provides a back-up in case of major problems. The engine problems with the F100 were finally solved after an alternative fighter engine, the General Electric F110, had been ordered in quantity. In the case of the ATF, the Air Force planned to develop two engines and test both extensively before choosing one engine to power all its aircraft.

ATF engines

The ATF engine was initially known as the Joint Advanced Fighter Engine (JAFE), because it was hoped to use it on the Navy's multi-role VFMX project. However, VFMX was dropped before the JAFE program had gone very far; the engine was at first known as the AFE and later as the ATF Engine (ATFE).

General Electric and Pratt & Whitney were awarded $550 million contracts to develop the ATF engines in September 1983. First, the two companies would build two prototype engines which would be internally representative of the final engine but need not be suitable for flight. The prototypes would be followed by flight-weight engines representative of the production design. These would undergo preliminary flight

rating tests (PFRT) and accelerated mission testing (AMT), a punishing sequence of tests intended to simulate a lifetime of service use in a few months of intensive running. (In 1983, the Air Force did not intend to fly the engines; they would be tested on the ground at Tullahoma.) General Electric's engine bore the in-company designation GE37, and was numbered F120 by the Air Force; the Pratt & Whitney design, the PW5000, received the Air Force designation F119.

The decision to fly prototypes put some pressure on the engine programs because the engines would have to be fully flight-qualified (which meant passing a further series of tests) before the aircraft could fly. Additional flight-test engines were authorized, and the schedule was re-arranged to qualify the engines quickly, before the completion of AMT. The prototype engines, the XF119 and XF120, made their first runs in late 1986. Lessons from these tests (General Electric's two engines ran 300 hours each, before they were retired in early

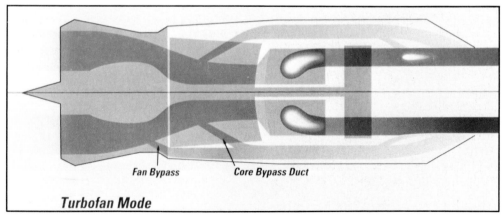

Fan Bypass   Core Bypass Duct

Turbofan Mode

The dual-cycle feature of the F120 is shown here. At maximum power (upper half of drawing) the fan bypass duct is closed, leaving only a small "leak" of air from the core to *cool the surrounding structure. The fan duct opens to reduce fuel consumption for subsonic cruise.* General Electric

1989) were applied to the YF119 and YF120 flight-weight engines, which were first run in late 1988.

Both ATF engines are powerful by any standards, delivering about 35,000 pounds of sea-level static thrust with full afterburner. Military power is about 23,500 pounds, some thirty-five percent more than the latest versions of the F100 and F110, but the difference between the two generations is even greater than these figures suggest. Because the bypass ratio of the ATF engine is low, the core provides nearly all the military power, so the cores are fifty to sixty percent bigger than the cores of today's engines. If the ATF engine cores were built into an engine with an F100's cycle, it would develop more than 40,000 pounds of augmented thrust.

The ATF engines are shorter than the F100 and F110, both because they have fewer stages and because the core exhaust is so hot that the fuel sprayed into the afterburner will auto-ignite in a distance of inches. The afterburner is shorter and simpler. Both engines can be equipped with fixed two-dimensional nozzles, for the YF-23, and vectoring nozzles for the YF-22. Even though they have heavier nozzles and produce more power than the F110 and F100, the ATF engines are of roughly equal weight.

F119

Details of the engines were restricted at the time these words were written. Pratt & Whitney's F119-PW-100 is believed to be the more conventional of the two. It is described as a turbofan, but with a very low bypass ratio of 0.2:1. The bypass ratio was chosen so that the augmentor has the cool, oxygen-rich air that it needs to generate the extra thrust required for acceleration, supersonic maneuver and Mach 2–plus dash performance.

F120

The General Electric F120 is different, being the first variable-cycle engine (VCE) to fly. It is a double-bypass engine; air is taken out of the compressor at two points. The first, larger bypass duct takes air from the low-pressure compressor; the second, smaller duct starts midway along the high-pressure compressor. The smaller duct is fixed, and bypasses just enough air to cool the rear end of the engine and feed the augmentor; the larger duct can be closed. Variable guide vanes throughout the engine, and a nozzle which can vary the relative bypass duct and core exit areas, adapt the engine to the flow changes.

For take-off, acceleration and supersonic flight, the forward bypass valve is closed, and the F120 operates as a high-pressure-ratio turbojet. The bypass duct is opened to improve specific fuel consumption for the subsonic cruise and loiter segment of the ATF mission. Pratt & Whitney says that its VCE studies have shown that cost, weight and complexity offset the performance advantages. General Electric has claimed better performance and, particularly, more military power at supersonic speed; the company believed its claims were vindicated in November 1990, with the Mach 1.58 flight of the YF-22.

Another unusual feature of the F120 is that its two shafts rotate in opposite directions. Because there are only two turbine stages, one for each shaft, there is no need for any fixed vanes to bend the airflow between the stages; this, says General Electric, shortens the turbine (the entire unit is only some seven inches long), reduces the parts count and saves on cooling air.

Two-dimensional nozzles

Both engines feature two-dimensional (2D) nozzles. Because of the very high pressure ratios of the ATF engines, together with the importance of efficient operation over a very wide speed range, both the throat and the final nozzle are independently variable. Today's variable convergent/divergent nozzles vary both areas with their curved, translating petals, but the relationship between them is fixed by the shape of the nozzle: for a given throat area there is a corresponding nozzle area. For best thrust, particularly with high pressure ratios (and correspondingly large expansion ratios across the nozzle), it is best to schedule both independently based on thrust, speed and altitude, which means a hinge at the throat. This is easier to mechanize with a 2D nozzle than with a conventional round shape. Given a 2D nozzle with an independently variable throat and exit, adding vec-

tored thrust is not too difficult, although some way must be found of taking the vertical loads into the airframe.

On the YF-23, the external part of the nozzle is formed by a single movable ramp above the exhaust and a fixed, curved ramp beneath it. On the YF-22, both external ramps move symmetrically, to vary the nozzle area, and differentially, to vector the exhaust stream.

Low-maintenance design

The ATF engines should also need less minor maintenance and should be easier to fix when something does go wrong. According to Brian Brimelow, manager of General Electric's F120 program, the more mundane side of the design has been handled better than it was in earlier programs. "For the first

Two-dimensional nozzles are heavier and harder to cool than round nozzles, but are mechanically simpler and allow vectoring and control of the exhaust plume shape.

They also permit a cleaner, more efficient afterbody or boat-tail design, particularly for a twin-engined aircraft. Lockheed

time," he says, "we said that we wanted high reliability, so that we would do the minimum amount of work on the engine. We have done a much better job on the parts of the engine which are not scientifically glamorous: tubes, wires, actuators and pumps, the sort of thing that you used to pass to a new engineer just out of school. We have taken the three-dimensional analysis techniques that we use on turbomachinery and applied them to tubes."

The F119 and F120 are also designed so that most components can be reached or removed while the engine remains on the aircraft. Locking wires have been eliminated, the number of different tools required to maintain the engine has been reduced, and the weight of individual accessory modules has been kept under thirty pounds so that one person can remove them unaided. "We have applied advanced technology," says Brimelow of the F120, "to make this engine something that is not a Tinker-toy."

Long before the ATF enters service, the engines will be run through thousands of simulated flight cycles to prove

their durability. The value of intensive testing was learned in the F100 program. Recent F100 and F110 derivatives have undergone accelerated mission testing, which simulates 4,000 fighter sorties in just over 1,000 hours of ground running; in effect, this puts the engine through half a lifetime of wear in a few months.

Early production examples of the newer versions have been selected for intensive use by operational squadrons, so that they accumulate hours much faster than the rest of the fleet and, in theory, unearth any unexpected problems in time for them to be put right. The aim is for the ATF engine to match or surpass the latest F100 and F110 fighter engines, which run for 4,000 cycles between major inspections.

In the late 1990s, the ATF will enter service with an engine that has been under development for over fifteen years and which has already flown through several operational lifetimes in ground testing. It will be about as far from the pilot's nightmare—an untried engine in an untried aircraft—as it is possible to get.

Chapter 4

The Mach 2 computer revolution

Radio aids contain boxes with coils. I don't like boxes with coils.

—Reichsmarschall Hermann Goering

Many pilots and more than a few airframe and engine designers harbor a sneaking sympathy for *Der Dicke*'s distrust of electrons and the devices which they inhabit. As Goering discovered, though, anyone in aerospace ignores or underestimates electronics at their peril.

The B-1 program showed how badly things can go wrong when the challenges of electronic systems are underrated. First, the development of the ALQ-161 electronic countermeasures (ECM) system for the original B-1A was started much later than the rest of the system. It had barely begun when the program was shelved. When the B-1 was resurrected in 1981, the political managers wanted the bomber operational as soon as the first squadron of aircraft could be built. The immense ALQ-161 had to be developed almost from scratch, put in a B-1B, tested and made operational in less than five years. The result was a mess that is still being disentangled as these words are written.

So far, the development of the ATF avionics has been run much better. This is not to say that there are not risks in prospect. Properly functioning electronics are critical to the ATF's mission. While the ATF avionics system arguably represents the way airborne electronics should be designed, many established ways of doing things (most of which were, at least, known to work) have been tossed out of the window.

Maintenance

A charge which is commonly leveled against US weapons is that they are unreliable and take too long to repair when they do fail. The charge has some substance, for two reasons. One is that each generation of aircraft has had more built-in features (such as internal ECM and inertial navigation) than the last, so that improvements in the reliability of individual systems tend to be offset by their greater number. The other problem is that the design of many of these devices has been driven, in its early stages, by performance alone. Questions such as reliability (how often will it fail?), availability (will it work when it is turned on?) and maintainability (what will it cost to fix?) were left until the detail design stage.

For the ATF, stiff requirements were set from the start for parameters such as maintenance manhours per flight hour (MMH/FH), mean time between maintenance actions (MTBMA) and turnaround time between sorties. The Air Force also wanted to reduce the amount of specialized equipment that a fighter wing requires in order to sustain operations.

Manpower was also a factor. Projections of Air Force recruitment in the 1990s and 2000s showed a declining military-age population and tougher competition from private industry in the labor market. This not only placed a premium on reducing MMH/FH, but pushed the Air Force to require that ATF should need fewer groups of specially trained people to maintain it. To support an F-15 wing, the Air Force

The ATF avionics system is built around high-performance common modules such as these. The modules are rugged and easily replaceable. Unisys

uses people trained in each of twenty-five specialized tasks; the goal for the ATF was to simplify those tasks so that between eight and ten specialties could cover all of them.

Another basic change required by the Air Force was two-level maintenance. There are now three levels: line, intermediate and depot. Line maintenance is done on the flight line. Aircraft of the F-15 generation are designed so that they can be quickly made available for a mission by removing a faulty component, such as part of the radar, and replacing it with a sound one; this is why avionics boxes are called line-replaceable units or LRUs.

At one time, anything that could not be repaired by the flight-line crew was packed up and sent back to one of the main Air Logistics Centers for depot-level maintenance, where it was checked by the best available equipment and, if necessary, completely remanufactured before it was reissued to the line.

As aircraft became more complicated and their parts became more expensive, this two-level system became impractical, because a tactical unit could not stock and carry enough replacements for every part. Intermediate level maintenance was introduced at each base, and shops were provided where faulty LRUs could be diagnosed and fixed by changing circuit cards.

With the F-15, intermediate maintenance expanded tremendously. A seventy-two-aircraft F-15 wing cannot sustain operations for more than a few days without its Avionics Intermediate Shop (AIS), which takes 130 people to run it. If the wing has to move to another base, the test equipment and spares which comprise the AIS fill four C-141 cargo aircraft: a quarter of the wing's support load.

Avionics modules

Rather than tinker with the problem, the Air Force has tackled it by changing the way that avionics systems are built. This is one more change which has been made possible by advances in computing. Specifically, the ATF avionics system is based on very high-speed integrated circuit (VHSIC) devices, of the kind which provide the motive power for high-speed personal computers and other electronic devices. VHSIC has made high-speed computers small, rugged and relatively inexpensive, and this is the cornerstone of the new approach to avionics which the Air Force developed in the early 1980s, under a demonstration program called Pave Pillar.

When electronic devices started appearing onboard aircraft, they functioned quite separately and their functions were integrated by the crew. Gradually, more of the devices were made to talk to each other; the radar was used to correct the navigation system, for example. By the 1970s, the Pentagon had imposed common formats for the information produced by each subsystem, so that they could be linked by a common databus rather than by a snake-pit of one-to-one connections. However, they were still independently developed and designed, and each LRU onboard the aircraft was different from all the others.

Consider this analogy: the aircraft was like an office with a smart telephone system, memory typewriters, a facsimile machine, a punch-card system for employee records and a computer for inventory control. If all these devices can be replaced by personal computers, running different programs, the office's work can continue even if one breaks down, because its programs and functions can be transferred to another one. Peripher-

The YF–22 avionics bay door (carrying the F–22 logo in this photo) is easily accessible from ground level. Inside, on the production ATF, will be a rack built into the aircraft, with space for 60 or more modules. There is another bay on the opposite side of the aircraft. Tony Landis

Rarely depicted mock-up of the ATF active array, including 1,500–plus transmit/receive modules. Bill Sweetman

als such as printers, scanners and optical character readers can be shared, saving money. When better computers are available, the office can be gradually upgraded by adding better but downwardly compatible equipment. When new peripherals appear, such as a combination scanner, character reader, fax and laser printer, the office is ready for them. All the time, the office manager can use quantity as a lever to reduce the price on computers.

Pave Pillar has done the same for the avionics system, replacing all the specialized computers and processors in the avionics system with VHSIC modules which, like the desktop computers, can be programmed to perform any one of many tasks. They can be reprogrammed in flight to replace another module which has failed, or to provide extra processing power for a function which requires it for only part of the mission.

Pave Pillar led to the formation of the Joint Integrated Avionics Working Group (JIAWG, pronounced *jye-wig*), an Air Force/Navy/Army group which has established common module specifications for the three services. JIAWG modules will be used on the Army's LH light helicopter as well as on the ATF, and will be used for future Navy aircraft (although the A-12 Avenger II strike aircraft was developed too early to be a JIAWG design). There is also no reason why identical modules should not be used on Army fighting vehicles.

The JIAWG modules are just over six inches square and a little more than half-an-inch thick. They are solid devices, weighing about one-and-a-half pounds, and will withstand all kinds of abuse which would cripple one of today's LRUs. There are several module types for different generic tasks, including digital data processors, analog-to-digital signal processors, bulk memory units, databus controllers and power supplies.

VHSIC provides very high performance. The ATF system is estimated to require a total throughput of 200 million instructions/second (mips) of data processing and 10 billion operations per second (bops) from the signal processors, which are designed to decode the stream of received energy from the radar or ECM in real time. The ATF system will need to store 200 megabytes (MB) of programs and data.

This is a great deal of information, even divided among many modules. The Hughes Common Integrated Processors being developed for the Lockheed team are each rated at 450 mips, a speed which was previously associated with supercomputers. All the modules incorporate their own built-in-test (BIT) systems and are programmed in Ada.

The modules slot into a rack that is built into the aircraft and provides them with raw power (conditioned and regulated by the power supply module) and cooling. The backplane of the rack incorporates high-speed fiber-optic linkages which allow the modules to communicate among one another much more quickly than today's LRUs, an essential foundation for the highly integrated way in which the different systems operate.

The JIAWG modules are liquid-cooled—the slots into which they fit are cooled, and conductive elements in the modules draw heat from the circuits into the slots—and run 55 deg F cooler than the air-cooled LRUs on current aircraft. This alone is claimed to make them last ten times longer. The modules are designed so that they can be removed from their racks, without tools, by an operator wearing full chemical, biological, radiation (CBR) protective gear.

The rack itself is simple and robust, and rarely requires removal.

The individual modules are designed to have an MTBF of several thousand hours. They cost about $30,000 each, but increases in production volume are expected to bring the figure down to $10,000 or less. Because a handful of common module types can replace four times as many different types of LRUs, and because they are reliable, many fewer spares are needed to support a fighter wing, and it can sustain operations without a large Avionics Intermediate Shop.

The Pave Pillar approach affects the entire avionics system, including the sensors. The ATF does not have a separate radar system in the same way as an F-15 does. Instead, the radar antenna is regarded as one of a number of apertures, along with the electronic warfare system and (if it is fitted later) the infrared search and track system. Signals from these apertures are processed by a bank of JIAWG-type common signal processors, which extract target returns and provide target data to the main mission processor, the display processor and the rest of the avionics system. What is important is that the pilot does not see an EW target and a radar target; the display shows only one.

The less glamorous but essential communication, navigation and identification (CNI) functions get the same treatment. Today's fighters have sixteen separate CNI devices, including navigation and landing beacon receivers, voice radios, identification friend-or-foe (IFF) and tactical datalinks. ATF uses Integrated CNI Avionics (ICNIA), which replaces all these LRUs by common antennas and JIAWG signal and data processors. ICNIA is also more reliable and takes up less than half the weight and volume of the classic CNI suite.

The combination of active jammers, passive radar-detectors and other devices used on current aircraft will be replaced on the ATF by the Integrated Electronic Warfare System (INEWS). Like ICNIA, INEWS will consist of a radio-frequency group, receivers and transmitters, linked to JIAWG common signal processors and controlled by JIAWG modules.

Other common modules belong to the vehicle management system (VMS) which embraces navigation, flight and propulsion control functions and manages the internal systems such as the fuel and environmental control system (ECS). Position and attitude sensing for flight control, navigation and mission management is provided by a novel inertial sensor including multiple ring-laser gyros (RLGs) in a fault-tolerant system

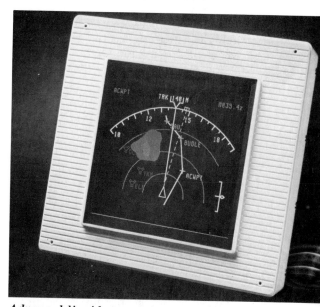

Advanced liquid crystal displays make it possible to put large-format, full-color, high-resolution displays in a fighter cockpit. Honeywell

which can continue to run with undiminished safety margins even after an error has been detected.

Active-array radar

The most radical of the ATF sensors, or apertures, is the radar array, which is being developed for both teams by Texas Instruments and Westinghouse. Radar is vital to a modern fighter but is one of its more trouble-prone components, mainly because of the high and rapidly fluctuating electrical power in its transmitter. The antenna's electrical drive system is also a source of problems. The ATF radar, which is descended from a project called the Ultra-Reliable Radar (URR), eliminates both the high-power transmitter and the antenna drive.

The ATF has not one radar, but thousands. Its active array consists of several thousand radar transmit/receive (T/R) modules, each about the size of one's finger, embedded in a flat liquid-cooled support structure with their tiny circular antennas pointing forward. Each T/R module contains a phase-shifter, a transmitter, a receiver and a pre-amplifier built into a single chip. The radar beam is steered by adjusting the phase of the T/R modules from one edge of the array to another, so that they transmit an oblique wave front.

The active array is not the same as the electronically steered array that is

This pictorial-format cockpit display was developed by Lockheed under the Pilot's Associate program. Stores management and navigation workloads are substantially reduced when displays like these, which are instantly comprehensible, replace indicator lights and alphanumeric formats. USAF

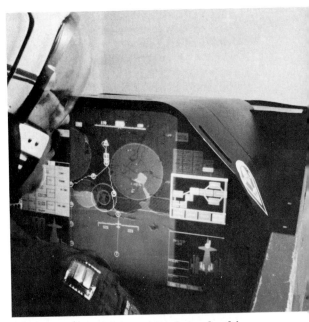

YF–23 team thinking may be shown by this display, produced for the Pilot's Associate program by McDonnell Douglas. The large central display is based on a digital map. Overlays on the map show the pilot's own track, the location and course of other aircraft, and the location and detection and lethal zones of surface-to-air missiles. USAF

used on the B-1. The latter has a single transmitter and receiver, and the beam is steered by phase-switchers in the physically fixed array. However, the two types do share some advantages. In particular, the beam can be pointed from one spot to another almost instantaneously. This makes it possible for the radar to switch from one mode to another so rapidly that it seems, in effect, to work in two or more modes at the same time; for instance, it can easily track almost any number of targets, over its entire field of view, while searching for others. The very rapid beam steering allows the antenna to hop from one target to another, dwelling on each long enough to resolve ambiguities and searching at high speed between dwells: "You can put the energy where it's needed," comments an engineer working on one active system.

Where the active array beats the electronically steered array, however, is in reliability. Even if several T/R modules fail, it will be almost unimpaired. The reliability target in the original URR program was an MTBF of 400 hours. The system's fault tolerance target was to demonstrate that it could operate from an austere base for thirty days, flying six 2.5 hour sorties per day, with a ninety percent probability of being capable of performing its mission by the end of that time.

The active-array radar has some inherent performance advantages. It should be very sensitive. Conventional radars suffer from losses in the outbound signal, between the transmitter and the antenna, and weak returns can be lost in the noise between the antenna and the receiver, but these sources are practically eliminated in the active array because the path between the transmitter, receiver and antenna is very short. Active arrays can be divided into sepa-

rate or overlapping sub-apertures, possibly with different waveforms or pulse repetition frequencies. These can be used to resolve ambiguities in the return and can allow the radar to operate in unusual modes.

The most important areas for improvement in fighter radars are non-cooperative target recognition (NCTR) and low probability of intercept (LPI). NCTR is the ability to confirm a contact as hostile beyond visual range; LPI is the radar designer's equivalent of Stealth. Most techniques in these areas are classified, but both are important and they go together, because the objective is for the ATF pilot to identify and engage his

Kaiser Electronics' Agile Eye helmet weighs less and is better balanced than the standard Air Force helmet, meets all protection requirements and includes a built-in helmet-mounted display. A miniature CRT is mounted in the back of the helmet, and a computer-designed chain of mirrors and lenses carries the image over the top of the pilot's head and projects it on a holographic screen built into the visor. Kaiser Electronics

target outside visual range and before being detected.

Although all military aircraft carry IFF equipment for identification, it will not be reliable in battle. A target with no IFF code may be a friendly with an inoperative IFF. NCTR technology aims to improve the radar image to the point where the pilot can identify aircraft types beyond visual range. One technique, useful against head-on targets, is to analyze the Doppler shift of the radar return for a regular undertone caused by the compressor blades of the target's engine. Another is to illuminate a target with a very rapid series of frequency-modulated (FM) radar pulses, so that the return has an extremely fine range resolution that can help to build up an image of the target.

Inverse synthetic aperture radar (ISAR) processing uses the Doppler shifts caused by rotational movement of the target relative to the radar to provide data from which a high-resolution image can be produced; it has mainly been discussed in public as a way of identifying ships, but there is no reason why it should not be used on aircraft. ATF radar supplier Texas Instruments is probably the leading exponent of ISAR.

The objective of LPI is, first, to prevent signals from being intercepted by hostile electronic surveillance systems and, if that fails, to ensure that they will be dismissed as noise. LPI techniques include power management, adjusting the power of the radar so that it is emitting no more energy than absolutely necessary, and "agility" in both frequency and waveform, so that the radar rapidly changes its characteristics from one pulse to the next. The active array, with its low-loss, low-noise characteristics, contributes to LPI by reducing the required power. Its ability to form several beams might also be used to perform several radar modes simultaneously, in one burst of power, compressing the radar's functions into a short time period and defeating attempts to track it.

Active-array radars can use novel electronic counter-countermeasures (ECCM) or anti-jamming techniques. The ability to concentrate radar energy on a target provides very strong burn-through performance; as its name implies, this means placing so much energy on the target that the real return overwhelms any deceptive signal. If the active array is faced with continuous-wave noise jamming, it is possible to use a few TR modules to transmit a null signal—half a phase out—directly toward the jammer, canceling the jamming signal.

An active array can also be split up physically, or extended. Small groups of

Lockheed's mock-up F–22 cockpit display aboard the Boeing 757 flying laboratory. Note the side-stick, which may have been selected to provide the largest possible clear, unobstructed panel space. The central, lower display is a touch-screen control panel. Lockheed

modules can be installed in the tail, wingtips, top and underside of the aircraft. The aim is not to turn ATF into an AWACS: the auxiliary arrays would not match the range or multi-mode capability of the main array. They could, however, track an enemy in a dogfight even when he is out of the pilot's field of view, and indicate where the hostile is likely to be when he does appear; they could also measure the range and speed of a target outside the field of view of the main array, allowing the fire-control system to determine whether the target can be hit with an off-boresight missile shot. Auxiliary arrays are not part of the baseline ATF, but are certainly being considered for future upgrades to it.

T/R modules

Technologically, the key to the active array is the ability to produce small, reliable T/R modules at a reasonable price. The modules are integrated circuits, like computer chips, except that they transform electrical power into microwave-frequency energy and back. Silicon-based circuits require too much energy and get too hot at high microwave frequencies, although they can be used at longer wavelengths. What makes the ATF radar possible is that its microwave monolithic integrated circuit (MIMIC) devices are made from gallium arsenide (GaAs), which can operate in the X-band (about 10 Ghz) used by fighter radars. Each module can generate about 10 watts of average power and should run for an average of 2,500 hours between failures.

The prototype modules used on the Dem/Val ATF radars cost up to $12,000 each, but it stands to reason that a fighter with a target flyaway cost of $43 million cannot afford to have $20 million worth of components in its radar antenna alone.

In parallel with the radar development, a Texas Instruments/Westing-house team and a General Electric/Hughes Radar Systems Group consortium are working on highly automated manufacturing technology to mass produce T/R modules in the same way that computer chips are produced. Texas Instruments has a target cost of $400. Once the module's cost drops much below $400, there is no point in trying to repair it; the unit will be tightly sealed during manufacture and thrown away if it fails.

Part of the MIMIC strategy is to expand the use of MIMICs into other radio-frequency systems, such as communications devices and electronic warfare systems, because the more MIMICs are used, the cheaper they get. Hughes, which is owned by General Motors, is working on MIMIC production technology with sister division Delco, and the automotive giant is not just thinking of ATF. A single T/R module could be part of a $100 option which would take the guesswork out of parallel parking.

The radar will be backed up by INEWS, which is intended to play an important role in locating and identifying threats which emit radiation. (It is also useful in identifying friendlies.) The systems which INEWS brings together will include sensitive and accurate antennae, capable of locating the bearing of a received signal within less than one degree; infra-red detectors which can detect missile launches or, at relatively close range, other aircraft; expendable decoys; and jammers. The jammer transmitters will use the same MIMIC technology as the radar, and will be built into the skin of the aircraft. Stealth and jamming are synergistic technologies, in that one helps the other work better. The smaller radar signature of a Stealth aircraft requires less jamming power to mask it, so the transmitters can be smaller and less powerful.

Another sensor originally planned for ATF was the infra-red search and track (IRST) sensor. Martin-Marietta leads General Electric in supplying an IRST for the YF-23; General Electric leads Martin-Marietta on the YF-22 effort. The IRST is designed to detect and track aircraft targets without any radar emissions. However, tests during Dem/Val showed that it was more difficult than expected for IRST to detect targets at a useful range, consistently, against a background of clutter; the Air Force has removed it from the baseline ATF but is continuing to work on the technology.

The ATF's active and passive sensors suck up an enormous volume of information over a range of at least 100 miles in all directions. In a dense combat environment, this 31,000-square-mile area can hold literally hundreds of airborne and ground-based threats and emitters. At the ATF's cruising speed, another 10,000 square miles comes into view every six minutes.

ATF cockpit

It is the task of the cockpit designer to ensure that the pilot can handle all this information without becoming "task-saturated," or so overloaded with data that he cannot absorb any more and may not be able to recognize even an urgent threat.

The F/A-18 pioneered the current generation of fighter cockpits, with five-inch monochrome cathode-ray tube multifunction displays (MFDs) replacing many of the dials and switches found on earlier aircraft. This was a vast improvement, but it still has limitations. The entire MFD area is smaller than the screen of a desktop computer. Each MFD can display only the output of one sensor, and different displays (such as navigation, radar and radar warning) are to different scales and viewed from different perspectives: for example, the radar display has the aircraft at the bottom, and is distorted to fit the conical scan on a square screen, while the radar-warning display has the aircraft at its center.

The YF-23 team's flying laboratory was a BAC One-Eleven transport which has been used to test Westinghouse radars since the 1970s. A Dem/Val model of the radar was installed in the nose, with EW receivers above it and the IRST underneath. The large pack on the fuselage side houses cooling equipment for the avionics. McDonnell Douglas

Fused displays

The ATF will feature "fused" displays in which the output of different sensors will be adjusted to a common scale and perspective and displayed on the same screen. This will require complex processing to ensure that the same target detected by two sensors is not displayed twice and that two targets which are close together are not incorrectly fused into one. The intention is that the system should be "sensor-transparent" to the pilot, who will see targets on his display rather than radar or IRST tracks. The pilot is not going to be monitoring the operation of the radar, but "will spend his time planning his attack, deciding who he's going to shoot first and how he's going to get out of Dodge City," ATF program manager Brig. Gen. James A. Fain has said.

Pictorial formats will be used, with instantly recognizable symbols and visual cues rather than letters, numbers and runes. On one display, the aircraft's track is overlaid on a map, together with the location of active and pre-briefed threats. Symbols will pulse or change color to reflect a change in status.

Such displays must be bigger than today's CRTs, and in full color. This, in itself, presents challenges. Color CRTs are inherently deeper in relation to their screen size than monochrome tubes, so large-format color CRTs, which are used on many new commercial aircraft, are too bulky and heavy for a fighter. Fighter displays also have to be very bright, because they must be readable even with sunlight falling directly on the screen. The ATF teams have pushed the state of the art in displays, and at least one—Lockheed—has chosen advanced liquid-crystal display (LCD) technology with backlighting and electronically switchable color filters.

The Lockheed cockpit uses screens originally developed by General Electric (although the technology has since been sold to France's Sextant); a full-color screen, 6.25 inches square, is less than three inches thick (a CRT with the same screen size would be fourteen inches deep). The crystals in the screen are sandwiched between two glass plates, and are individually switched from opaque to transparent in 100,000 zones by thin-film transistors formed on the inside surfaces of the plates. The screen combines high contrast with 320x320 pixel resolution and is brighter than a CRT. While LCDs are inherently monochromatic, the unit is fitted with red, green and blue filters on its face. The display presents a full-color image by showing red, green and blue images in rapid succession and is back-lit in intense sunlight.

The YF–22 cockpit uses an eight-inch-square full-color tactical situation display, and two six-inch-square displays dedicated to attack management and EW. Two three-color LCD displays are used for stores and systems management. Lockheed may have chosen a side-stick controller, so as not to block any part of the display space.

Helmet-mounted display

The ATF will have a head-up display (HUD). It is an open question, however, whether it will have a helmet-mounted display (HMD). Lockheed refers to it as a growth item. The HMD consists of a miniature CRT and a chain of lenses attached to the helmet, which project data on the pilot's visor. A head-movement tracker monitors where the pilot is looking, both relative to the aircraft and to the outside world.

The HMD has many potential uses. It can help the pilot spot a target detected by the radar or the INEWS that is outside the field of view of the HUD. An arrow shows the pilot where to look, and when the target is in the HMD field a box appears over it. The pilot can use the HMD to designate a target for a missile, making the best use of off-boresight weapons. A simple space-stabilized, line-of-sight display in the HMD allows one pilot to cue his wingman on to a target. "135 degrees, 45 up" is much more specific than "three o'clock, high" and is not referenced to the direction of one aircraft. As long as the distance between the pair is a fraction of the distance to the target, the second pilot should be able to look in the right direction and acquire the target quickly.

Going into an engagement, a pilot will normally look at a target, lock the radar onto it and look around for potential threats; then he must look out again to re-acquire his target for a visual attack. With the cueing indicator on an HMD, re-acquisition is much easier, particularly at the limits of visual range.

In August 1987, the Kaiser Electronics Agile Eye helmet, with a built-in HMD, was tested in an HMD dome simulator in one-versus-one manned combat simulations. The results were remarkable. The kill-to-loss ratio against the same threat doubled from 1.8:1 to 3.8:1. Pilots fired twice as many AIM-9 Sidewinders with the HMD as without it. Even if the non-HMD pilot saw his adversary first, the pilot with the HMD often took the first shot. One pilot involved in the tests was quoted as saying: "Who do we have to shoot to get this thing?"

The fact that the HMD is not part of the ATF program does not reflect a lack of interest by the Air Force. Because the HMD can be used on all fighters and is basically a plug-in device, it may not make sense to tie its development to a specific aircraft. There are also some

technical issues to be resolved. Agile Eye represented one approach to the problem of keeping the HMD light and compact. There are, however, strong arguments against building part of the avionics system into a piece of personal equipment, and the Air Force seems to favor a solution in which the HMD system is removable from the helmet and stays with the aircraft.

Adaptive aiding

More subtle changes to the cockpit may stem from a program called Pilot's Associate, which is being run independently of ATF, but by two teams which each include a member of one ATF team. (Lockheed is leading one, McDonnell Douglas the other.) Pilot's Associate is partly concerned with information fusion. However, it also includes a concept known as "adaptive aiding."

It is generally agreed that attempting to automate the fighter is a bad idea. Adaptive aiding is different, because it is intended to help the pilot according to an assessment of his needs. As the system detects that the pilot is becoming busier, dealing with more inputs and issuing more commands, it will gradually begin to automate more functions. For instance, it may assume control of defensive electronic warfare and chaff/flare systems in combat, or select and prepare weapons for firing if the pilot appears to be engaging a target. In order to do this, the system's software will be designed to learn from human experts, such as particularly skilled and proficient pilots, and to distill their responses into guidelines and rules which will allow the on-board computers to evaluate each unique situation and help the pilot make tactical decisions.

Pilot's Associate is not a fixed part of the ATF program, but since most of the program's product is in the form of software it can easily be transitioned into the Pave Pillar architecture.

Fighter software

The main challenge in the entire ATF avionics system resides in the software, which is being required to do far more of the work than it does on any other aircraft. The ATF needs more than two million lines of code, each of which must be right in order for the system to perform reliably.

The system uses a computer language called Ada. Engineers joke that "if architects built houses the way programmers write software, one woodpecker could destroy Western civilization." Ada, which has been adopted by the Pentagon for all military vehicle applications, is the response to this mean but not wholly inaccurate jab. Compared with languages such as Jo-

vial, which was previously used for many avionics systems, an Ada program is more efficient, and easier to design and integrate. Ada is modular, so that one part of a program can be redesigned without rewriting the rest of it. An Ada programmer can look at another's work in Ada, and see immediately what the other was doing.

The size and importance of the software package raise concerns about espionage or even sabotage. The software will contain an enormous amount of information about the aircraft and all its systems, and about US knowledge of an enemy's systems. In a nightmare scenario, ATF software could be corrupted by an undetectable "mole" which would shut down critical functions in response to a signal received by radar or INEWS. Information security (Infosec) has been

YF–22 team member Boeing usually has a spare airliner lying around somewhere. The first Boeing 757 was selected as the avionics laboratory, outfitted with radar, IRST and defensive systems in the nose and wingtips. Lockheed

applied throughout the ATF program, both through basic design concepts and the use of the KOV-5 Advanced Avionics COMSEC Unit, an encryption/decryption common module developed for the Air Force by the National Security Agency.

However, the sheer scope of writing that much software, and then testing and validating it so that it will function properly under the hard-to-simulate stresses of battle, is daunting and absorbs an enormous amount of time even if it is managed extremely well. In mid-1988, the Air Force asked its Scientific Advisory Board (SAB) to review the entire ATF avionics program. The SAB, which is a quasi-independent organization including veteran engineers, academics and consultants, carried out a detailed study, and developed more than fifty major findings that resulted in hundreds of changes to the ATF Dem/Val program. The overall conclusion, though, was that the risks involved in the highly integrated, software-dependent ATF system were manageable. The final decision, to commit to the new architecture for the FSD program, was made in late 1988.

Gen. Michael Loh, Aeronautical Systems Division commander, said in mid-1989, "There is no going back. As we can do more and more by software we do it that way. It's cheaper, and much easier to modify and upgrade...but it is a major problem in terms of meeting schedules."

In earlier programs, General Loh said, "Eighty percent of our software problems were uncovered during testing, and only twenty percent during the design stage. That's a level I can't stand. We must uncover eighty to ninety percent of the problems in design."

Prototype testing

The contract for the most important element of the Ultra-Reliable Radar (URR), the solid-state array, was issued to Texas Instruments as far back as April 1983. Despite the radical nature of the radar, the prototype was tested in 1988. By the time the ATF teams were ready to put radars in their Avionics Ground Prototype laboratories, Texas Instruments and Westinghouse were building second-generation products.

The ground laboratory testing is also an advance over previous avionics tests, which concentrated on individual systems and frequently failed to reveal problems of integration between systems. Again, ATF tests which have been done before FSD are, in many cases, more extensive than tests done during FSD in previous programs. The prototypes were not intended to run all the ATF software, but both have run more than 500,000 lines of code with some success. Overall, the objective was not to demonstrate the final FSD performance level, but to check the demonstrated performance of the prototypes against what their designers had predicted. If the prototypes performed roughly as expected, it meant that the design techniques for hardware and software had worked.

Both ATF teams also flew their avionics prototypes during Dem/Val, even though this was not a strict requirement. Both teams used airliners—Northrop and McDonnell Douglas used a BAC One-Eleven, leased from Westinghouse, and Lockheed's team used the first Boeing 757 prototype—because the objective was not to make a system work in a fighter, but to test its performance against real targets in free space, with real noise and clutter sources. In a ground laboratory, targets, noise and clutter are simulated by computer, and it is very difficult to be certain that differences between real and simulated targets are not significant. Both systems flew for about 100 hours in 1990, enough to validate the data gathered on the ground. In particular, tests against real targets showed that the system could detect a target by multiple sensors and display it reliably and consistently as one symbol on the pilot's display.

The winning team's prototype will be upgraded into a systems integration laboratory, and the flying prototype will become the Avionics Flying Test Bed (AFTB). The use of an AFTB has already shown its value on the B–2 program. By the time that a full-up avionics system is installed in an ATF full-scale development aircraft, the system should be tested and mature, and ready for final proof-of-performance testing.

Another important tool in the design of the ATF avionics and cockpit has been the flight simulator. Both teams built massive simulation facilities early in the program, allowing them to test displays and information systems with one pilot in the cockpit of the ATF and another in an adversary aircraft. The YF–22 and YF–23 cockpits should be user-friendly from the start.

The Air Force hopes that the ATF avionics will work better than earlier systems because of the enormous amount of work that has been done before the start of full-scale development. In fact, Gen. Lawrence A. Skantze, commander of the USAF Systems Command in 1987, disclosed at that time that the Air Force would spend $900 million on avionics during the ATF Dem/Val stage, more than on either the engine or the airframe, and that one contractor was estimating that avionics would account for forty percent of the fighter's fly-away cost ($14 million in 1985 money).

Chapter 5

Weapons for the supersonic dogfight

I told everyone I was going to demonstrate the synchronized gun that morning. No one would believe that it would operate successfully . . . I had not figured on the conservative military mind, which has not only to be shown, but then wishes to be shown all over again, after which it desires a little time to think the whole matter over once more.

—Anthony Fokker, inventor of the first practical forward-firing aircraft gun.

Like most of history's more successful aircraft, the ATF does not represent a radical departure from the past in the weapons that it carries. In fact, it may enter service with a missile designed in the 1950s and a gun dating back to the 1940s.

Truly radical solutions to the problems of arming the fighter have been tried from time to time, usually leading to disappointment or disaster. Many studies and tests had shown that the RAF's Defiant turret-armed fighter of 1940 would be an effective weapon, but they were lambs to the slaughter in the Battle of Britain. The bloody lesson that was learned is that there is no conclusive test of fighter weapons except combat.

Missiles

The all-missile fighters conceived in the 1950s, such as the F-102 and early F-4, were merely disappointing. The F-4 did better than most all-missile fighters in Vietnam, because it was big enough to carry four short-range air-to-air missiles (AAMs) in addition to the four medium-range missiles which it was originally designed to carry. The short-range Sidewinders would work at close quarters where the medium-range AAMs were too unwieldy to engage targets, and sheer numbers compensated for the poor probability of kill from a single shot. What was missing was the gun: in the chaos of a dogfight, F-4 pilots would come so close to the enemy that their missiles would overshoot the target before their safety arming and fusing devices could operate. Gun pods and the new F-4E, with an internal gun, were rushed into service.

The F-4's mix of two kinds of AAM and a gun has been compared to a rifle, a pistol and a boot-knife. Its key attribute is "graceful degradation": the weapon envelopes overlap, so the pilot never finds himself at grips with the enemy without usable weapons. The F-4's armament was adopted unchanged for the F–15 and has been retained for the ATF.

AMRAAM

The ATF's primary weapon will be the USAF/Hughes AIM-120 Advanced Medium-Range AAM (AMRAAM), which will also be carried by F–15s and F–16s and has been under development for much longer than the ATF itself. The AMRAAM has had a long and sometimes difficult evolution.

Nevertheless, several years behind schedule, AMRAAM appears to be emerging from its thicket of problems and some critical tests have been accomplished successfully. AMRAAM will be the main armament of the F–15 and it will arm the ATF into the foreseeable future. Because it has been adopted as a standard NATO weapon, it will also be carried by the F–16, the F–18, RAF Tornado interceptors, Royal Navy Sea Harriers and, beginning in 1995, the Eurofighter EFA.

AMRAAM will replace the AIM-7 Sparrow, which dates to the 1950s in its configuration and basic design. Sparrow looks very like AMRAAM: this is because the new missile was designed to fit AIM-7 stations with few changes. The AIM-7 weighs about 500 pounds and has fixed tailfins and movable wings for control; it flies at about Mach 3. The AMRAAM is lighter (about 320 pounds) and faster (around Mach 4). Its wings are fixed and the tail surfaces move.

Both missiles have a maximum launch range of about sixty miles, under ideal conditions—that is to say, with the targets closing head-on at high speed at the same altitude, so that the distance from launch to impact is less than the distance to the target at launch. If the missile has to chase the target from astern, or attack a maneuvering target from the side, the launch is only a fraction of the maximum value. AMRAAM is

faster and (thanks to its tail controls) more maneuverable than the AIM-7, so it is not quite as badly affected by non-optimum launch conditions.

The critical difference between the two is in their guidance systems. The AIM-7 is a semi-active radar homing (SARH) missile, which homes on to radar energy transmitted by the launch aircraft and reflected by the target. The shooter's radar must illuminate the

The eight-missile plus single cannon armament of the F-15 has become the baseline for ATF; the big difference is that the ATF weapons are carried internally. USAF

target continuously from launch until impact. As long as its radar is locked on to the target and illuminating, it cannot detect or track other targets. The pilot is therefore in the unpleasant position of running blindly toward the enemy until the missile hits the target.

AMRAAM is an active-radar homing (ARH) missile with a miniature radar, an inertial-navigation system (INS) and a datalink receiver, all connected to a central computer. The missile's radar cannot track the target at maximum range, so the fighter's fire-control computer predicts the target's position at impact and loads it into the missile's computer, just before it is fired. The AMRAAM uses INS data to steer toward that position. The shooter's radar continues to track the target as it maneuvers and changes speed, and, through the datalink, transmits the new impact point to the missile. Up to fifteen miles from the target, the missile's own radar locks on and guides the weapon to impact.

The attacker's radar is fully functional during the attack. The ability to track several targets while searching for others was built into the F-15 and F-14 radars, and the ATF's active array will be able to track maneuvering targets more reliably, over a larger area. Because the aircraft-to-missile datalink can be time-shared, the number of missiles which can be flying against different targets at the same time is limited by information processing power and the pilot's ability to acquire, identify, prioritize and attack targets in the time available. The ATF goal is a real four-on-four capability.

AMRAAM's homing system is extremely accurate, and because of the missile's tail control surfaces it can maneuver very rapidly close to the target, deriving lift from its ogival nose

and its body as well as from its wings. As a result, the missile can be expected to pass closer to the target, and the proximity-fused blast/fragmentation warhead can be made smaller; it probably weighs about forty to forty-five pounds, roughly half the mass of the AIM-7 warhead. This is why AMRAAM is slimmer and lighter—and hence faster—than the AIM-7.

AMRAAM has an alternative "launch-and-leave" mode that can be used if the target is within range of the missile's radar. Range in this mode is about fifteen miles, considerably less than the maximum, but radar guidance may give it a greater launch range and higher kill probability than a conventional short-range infra-red missile under some circumstances; in haze or cloud, for instance, or if the target is against the sun.

In computer-simulated combat against aircraft equipped with Sparrow (which can be taken as representative of semi-active weapons) aircraft armed with AMRAAM launched their weapons, guided them to the point where they became autonomous, and broke off before entering the lethal envelope of the AIM-7s launched by their opponents "under almost any scenario," according to the Air Force.

A drawback of AMRAAM is that it was designed in the late 1970s, before anyone believed that a Stealthy counter-air fighter could be developed. Nobody thought that it would ever be carried in an internal weapon bay, so it has large wings and fins which take up a great deal of room. Unclassified drawings of the production F-23A, for instance, show four AMRAAMs in a very large rear bay, and two short-range weapons in the forward bay: two missiles fewer than an F-15 and four fewer than the Sukhoi

Su–27. It is unlikely that this is the definitive configuration.

A compressed-carriage version of AMRAAM, with folding wings and fins, is almost certainly under development for ATF under a classified program. The mechanical task is not quite as simple as it sounds. The fins have to extend very quickly and lock into place in a Mach 2 airstream. There is also a reliability concern, because all eight fins must extend properly; even if the individual fins failed only once in 100 operations, this could mean that one launch in fifteen might fail from this cause alone. Compressed carriage would probably allow the ATF to carry up to ten missiles.

ASRAAM

Unclassified drawings show ATF being armed with AIM–9 Sidewinder missiles. The AIM–9 is a successful and reliable weapon, but its basic design is very old. A new missile could be more agile and would be able to attack targets off the aircraft's boresight. Such a missile, the AIM–132 ASRAAM (Advanced Short-Range Air-to-Air Missile), is under development by British Aerospace and Bodensee Geraten-Technik (BGT) of Germany until 1990, and was originally intended to replace the AIM–9 throughout NATO. Since 1988, however, the Air Force has been extremely cool toward the ASRAAM and has made no funds available to buy it.

It is possible that an AIM–9 replacement has been developed by the Air Force as a black program. It would use tail control, which, as in the case of AMRAAM, provides better maneuverability. It might also use vectored thrust, which is necessary to allow the missile to make fast, very large flightpath changes immediately after launch. This is useful if the target is at close range, and moving toward the launch aircraft or across its track. Vectored thrust is important if the launch aircraft is firing from a high angle-of-attack position, because, relative to the air, the missile is actually flying crabwise as it leaves the launch rail. With vectored thrust, the missile can pitch rapidly forward into a normal flight attitude, accelerate and then maneuver after its target.

A new short-range AAM would probably have an infra-red seeker working in both the midwave and long-wave bands to reduce its susceptibility to countermeasures, and an inertial-reference system.

AA-ARM

Another weapon that may have been developed under a black program is an air-to-air antiradiation missile (AA-ARM). One such weapon, the Hughes Brazo, was investigated in the early 1970s. As its name suggests, the AA-ARM would home on to the radar signals from a hostile aircraft. A pure AA-ARM could be easily spoofed if the target's missile-warning system spotted it in time and the target switched off its radar and pulled a hard break. Its operation could also be frustrated if the target used radar intermittently. The AA-ARM is likely to switch to an infra-red seeker as soon as the target is within range, to negate such countermeasures. Hardware for such a dual-mode version of the AIM–9 has been demonstrated.

Launching AAMs from an internal bay is a technology which has to be revived and updated rather than invented. In the 1950s, supersonic interceptors such as the General Dynamics F–102 and F–106 carried their Falcon AAMs internally. The missile launch rails were mounted on mechanical trapeze mechanisms which forced them clear of the airframe under positive control. Weapons were routinely fired at supersonic speed. The Air Force has recently tested a number of trapeze designs, probably intended for the ATF.

The Lockheed YF–12 launched missiles successfully at Mach 3, using small side-firing rockets on the nose and tail of the weapons to retain positive control. (Otherwise, Ben Rich recalled, "The missile always wanted to come up between the front and rear cockpits.") At high-g, however, rail launch is probably essential in order to ensure that the missile, if its motor ignites, goes nowhere but straight ahead.

AAAM

The Navy ATF will carry a wider range of weapons. For its primary fleet-air-defense mission, it will be armed with the Advanced Air-to-Air Missile (AAAM), the long-range replacement for the AIM-54 Phoenix. Two teams are competing to develop AAAM: General Dynamics/Westinghouse and Hughes/Raytheon (McDonnell Douglas is a major subcontractor to the latter). In late 1990, the program was in the middle of a four-year competitive Dem/Val program.

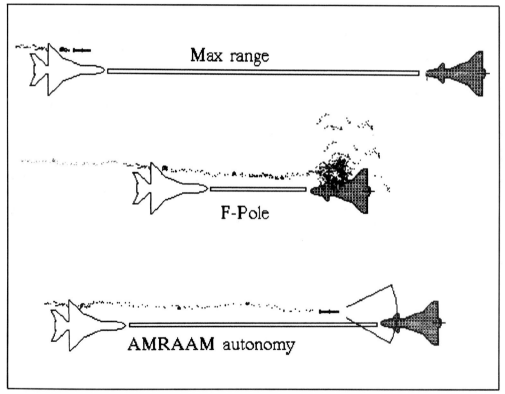

The maximum launch range of a semi-active missile (top) applies to a head-on missile duel. The shooter and the target will be separated by a much smaller distance, the F-Pole, when the missile hits and the shooter can look for other targets (middle). AMRAAM is faster, and its active radar makes it autonomous for the last section of its flight (bottom), so the launch aircraft is free to break much earlier. Bill Sweetman

AAAM will have a range of over 100 miles and is intended to be smaller and more lethal than Phoenix.

The Navy also wants its ATF to carry air-to-surface weapons for a back-up strike role: the AGM–88 High-Speed Antiradiation Missile (HARM), the AGM–84 Harpoon anti-shipping missile and the Advanced Interdiction Weapon System (AIWS) glide bomb.

Guns

ATF will carry an internal gun, and it will almost certainly be the General Electric Improved M61A1 20 mm, six-barrel Gatling cannon. More than forty years old in its basic design, the M61A1 has been proved lethal and reliable in many air combats. The most visible difference in the Improved M61A1 is that its barrels are longer (seventy-nine inches versus sixty inches) to increase its muzzle velocity. Less visible, lighter materials and component changes offset the weight increase due to the longer barrels.

The alternative to the Improved M61A1 is an all-new weapon based on the Advanced Gun Technology (AGT) program. AGT has produced prototype guns firing cased, telescoped (CT) ammunition, in which most of the propellant is loaded in the form of a cylinder around the projectile, rather than behind it. When the gun fires, an initiator pushes the projectile out of the case as the main charge fires. The main advantage is that tightly packed, consolidated propellants can burn as efficiently as looser propellant in an oversized case, increasing practical muzzle velocity without the problems of a large round. AGT was aimed at muzzle velocities around 5,000 ft/sec, compared with 3,600 ft/sec for the Improved M61.

The other advantage is that the CT round can be produced as a right circular cylinder (it is sometimes disrespectfully called the "beer-can round"). This shape can be stored much more efficiently than the traditional tapered, shouldered cartridge.

A flight-weight version of the AGT gun was successfully fired in 1989, but the cost and logistical complications of introducing a new gun will probably keep it off the ATF. The M61A1 may not offer such high performance, but its development costs are infinitesimal compared with those of a brand-new weapon. It uses the same ammunition as 5,000-plus US and allied fighters, and the AGT's main advantages are at longer ranges, where guns give way to AAMs.

All the ATF's weapons were designed against one yardstick: the threat posed by the Soviet Union. The AIM–120 was intended to give Western fighters the edge against the superior numbers of Warsaw Pact forces. The main role of the AAAM is to shoot down Tupolev Tu–22M Backfire bombers in the outer air battle, before they can launch missiles against US Navy carriers. By late 1990, this threat had changed enormously, leading many to wonder if the ATF would be needed at all.

Chapter 6

ATF and the 1989 revolution

War will exist as long as there's a food chain.

—*P. J. O'Rourke*, Holiday in Hell

When military and industry representatives gathered in Anaheim, California, next door to Disneyland, to talk about the ATF in October 1982, not one person present knew what would happen to the Soviet Union and the Warsaw Pact in the next eight years. Actually, if any genius or psychic had known what would happen, and had voiced a correct prediction, they would have been advised to look for a new line of work, probably involving a move across the road from the Anaheim Convention Center and a pair of mouse ears.

The Eastern European revolution of 1989 has wrought irreversible change. The post–1945 order is dead and buried. Europe east of the Elbe will no longer be part of a military machine taking orders from Moscow.

The Warsaw Pact threat dominated the thoughts of the people who wrote the ATF requirement; but it is not logical to conclude that the ATF is redundant because the Warsaw Pact is void.

Civilization starts when people agree on basic standards of behavior and form groups within which individual conflicts of interest can be averted or settled under law. Small groups form larger aggregations in the same way. The highest echelon of groups consists of nations, but since there is no higher authority than a nation, the rule of law is patchy. Disputes between nations of strongly differing values tend to be settled by force.

Nobody should have been too surprised when Iraq invaded Kuwait in August 1990. Iraq owed billions to Kuwait. Kuwait's armed forces were a pushover. If there is no law, there is nothing to stop you invading your bank to clear your overdraft.

The fact that lines of conflict are no longer aligned with the East/West divide does not mean that the world is stable. The Soviet Union itself is riddled with the fault-lines of war. Tsar Nicholas II ruled an empire, not a country; the Communists who killed him claimed that they presided over a union of Socialist republics, and fooled nearly everybody, including themselves. But the military, the KGB and centralized economic control have been instruments of empire, and as they decay, nationalism is beginning to stir. Anyone who claims to know what the world between Lvov and Vladivostok will look like in another eight years can go and line up for their mouse ears.

In the Middle East, religious and sectarian frontiers extend across the political borders which the map-makers like, into the Soviet Union and to the frontiers of the new Europe. The less the region is stable, the higher the price of oil, and the bigger the pay-off from aggression or extortion.

The time when nations do not need armed forces is a long way off, longer than the service life of a new class of airplane and much longer than the F–15 can reasonably be expected to last. The question is whether the ATF is now the best solution for the different military requirements of the next century.

The decision is critical because the ATF is not only the largest military program in prospect, but also one of the largest industrial projects of any kind in the United States. The original planned program cost, for the US Air Force's 750 aircraft, was $65 billion in "then-year" dollars: that is to say, the sum includes projected inflation up to the year in which the expense is incurred. The program cost includes full-scale development of the aircraft, including the engine and avionics, together with all the specialized equipment needed to support the aircraft and to train flight and maintenance crews. It does not include the money already spent on Dem/Val.

However, the $65 billion figure assumed that the ATF met the target flyaway cost—the average cost of one fully equipped ATF, excluding research, development and support costs—of $35 million in 1985 dollars. This was always dubious; the Air Force's best estimate in 1985, after three hard years of ATF studies, was $40 million. It also assumed that the ATF was to be built according to the

original plan, at a rate of seventy-two aircraft per year.

Under pressure to reduce the defense budget in early 1990, however, Defense Secretary Richard Cheney decided to decelerate the process of re-equipping the Air Force and Navy with Stealth aircraft. Under the Major Aircraft Review (MAR), announced in April 1990, ATF full-scale development (FSD) will still be launched in June 1991. However, the start of low-rate production was deferred two years, until 1996. ATF will now join the squadrons in 1998. The number of aircraft to be built each year will be forty-eight, rather than seventy-two; this rate will be reached in 2001.

Cutting the production rate raises the flyaway cost, for several reasons. Fixed facilities and tooling still cost the same, and it will be harder to achieve the desired reductions in the cost of avionics common modules and MIMIC chips. Stretching out the production program will increase the impact of inflation on the then-year costs (because costs will be incurred later in years of higher inflation). The total, then-year program cost will rise to between $80 billion and $90 billion.

Under the MAR, the Navy ATF (NATF) program was also deferred by two years. FSD will not start until 1994. Low-rate production will not be authorized until 1998, and the full planned rate, which has been reduced from forty-eight to thirty-six aircraft per year, will not be achieved until 2003.

The future of the NATF is far from certain. Adm. Richard Dunleavy, the US Navy's chief of aircraft requirements, said in August 1990 that he did not see how NATF could fit into any affordable plan for Navy aviation. Then, in January 1991, the Navy's top-priority A–12 medium attack aircraft was abruptly canceled due to massive weight, cost and

The Soviet Union builds 100 Sukhoi Su–27s per year. With the coming of glasnost, this extremely capable fighter is a regular at international air shows and is likely to be made available for export. Bill Sweetman

A larger-winged development of the F–16, the Agile Falcon, was proposed in 1987 as a complement to the ATF. General Dynamics

schedule overruns, throwing Navy plans back into the melting pot.

If NATF goes ahead, the total value of the ATF and NATF program is nearly doubled. The total cost of NATF is estimated at $58 billion in 1985 dollars, including $30.4 billion for the production of 546 aircraft (this indicates that the NATF will be more expensive than the ATF, with a flyaway cost of $50 million). Converting the then-year dollars and adding the USAF program, the total cost of ATF and NATF could be $175 billion. Even under the MAR reductions announced in April 1990, total peak production could be eighty-four aircraft per year by 2003, worth a total of several billion dollars.

Given the changes in the world since 1982, are there less costly alternatives to the ATF? The question here is whether the United States' defense still requires the capabilities of the ATF, or whether less capable and less expensive fighters, or a different force mix, would be more appropriate.

The least expensive option is to do virtually nothing; to assume that, with the end of the Cold War, the superpowers will cease the arms-technology race which came in with the industrial revolution. In that case, the argument runs, continued low-rate production of F–15s and F–16s, with minimal changes, will replace aircraft lost in accidents, and due to wear and tear, and provide a credible defense indefinitely.

One of the most significant flaws in this argument is that the defense of the United States and its allies has never relied on mere technological parity. Prosperous democracies are at a disadvantage compared with one-party states where the government runs the economy and the armed forces can be maintained on unlimited conscription. An all-volunteer force is smaller than a conscript army, and yet it costs as much or more in pay and benefits. Its advantage is that it is better trained, and can make better use of sophisticated weapons to prevail against the force of numbers.

Smaller forces need to have the technological edge, as has been seen in the Arab-Israeli wars and in the Falklands. In the counter-air mission, F-16s and F-15s—excellent as they are—do not provide the same margin of superiority over the MiG-29 and Su-27 as they asserted over the MiG-23.

In 1990, the Soviet Union was expected to build 150 MiG-29s and 100 Su-27s; the conversion of military aircraft factories to civil production has not affected these two types, only obsolescent designs such as the MiG-23 and Su-25.

The MiG-29 is a competent design and a well-armed aircraft. It has some inherent disadvantages compared with the F-15 and F-16, including inferior visibility and a poor cockpit design. However, it carries more weapons than the F-16, including what appears to be a very potent infra-red-homing missile, and it can be flown at very steep angles of attack. It has an infra-red search and track system.

The Su-27 is a different class of fighter, and it is a fair guess that it costs between 50 and 100 percent more to produce than the MiG-29. Of all fighters in production, East or West, it has the largest radar, the most power, the heaviest armament and the greatest internal fuel capacity. It is considered able to out-accelerate most current fighters, and its low-speed maneuverability, as

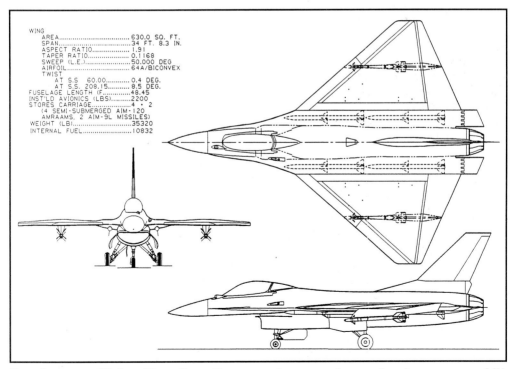

```
WING
  AREA..................................630.0 SQ. FT.
  SPAN..................................34 FT. 8.3 IN.
  ASPECT RATIO.................1.91
  TAPER RATIO.................0.1168
  SWEEP (L.E.)................50.000 DEG
  AIRFOIL...........................64A/BICONVEX
  TWIST
    AT S.S  60.00..........0.4 DEG.
    AT S.S. 208.15........8.5 DEG.
FUSELAGE LENGTH (F.......48.45
INST'LD AVIONICS (LBS)......2200
STORES CARRIAGE............4 · 2
  (4 SEMI-SUBMERGED AIM-120
  AMRAAMS, 2 AIM-9L MISSILES)
WEIGHT (LB)..........................35320
INTERNAL FUEL..................10832
```

One of a range of Falcon 21 configurations, this tailless, trapezoidal-wing design would *have superior speed and weapons capability to the current F-16.* General Dynamics

demonstrated at the 1989 Paris air show, is eye-popping: carefully developed fly-by-wire, vortex-control devices and powerful control surfaces take credit for that capability. The Soviet Union has built 620 Su-27s since the early 1980s, which is two-thirds the total of F-15 production since 1974.

Global trends will erode the edge which the F-16 and F-15 provide even if the entire Soviet realm converts en masse to Quakerism. The obvious trend is that the Soviet Union is keen to earn foreign exchange, as are all nations. Since the Soviet Union is not about to blow Sony or Honda out of world markets anytime soon, its planners have to promote sales of the goods in which they have invested most heavily over the past fifty years: military equipment. The Soviet Union's economic problems will make Soviet fighters, radars and SAMs available to almost any cash buyer.

However, it was not AS-4 Kitchen anti-ship missiles which sunk HMS *Sheffield* in the South Atlantic or crippled the USS *Stark* in the Gulf, but Exocet missiles from France. Military threats in a post-polarization world do not necessarily emanate from Soviet clients. They may come from former allies or non-aligned nations, some of them with the money to equip powerful armed forces.

Many of these nations, particularly the oil-producers and industrial powerhouses, are also enjoying the fruits of two decades of surplus income over expenses. In the 1970s, they began to send their best and brightest to the West's universities. In the 1990s, the nature of warfare and military power is changing as countries such as India, Iran, Iraq and Syria begin to reflect the development of technological elites. They can and will begin to develop their own weapons and improvements to existing systems.

A military/technical strategy based on stagnation is inherently slow to respond to change of this kind, and also inefficient; it is wasteful to bypass technology which can provide equivalent defense for less manpower and lower operating expenses. The last time this was tried, in the United States, was between 1918 and the mid-1930s. The results were felt in 1941.

A more realistic alternative to ATF is to modify current fighters to embody some ATF technology. A USAF "Red Team," in conjunction with McDonnell Douglas and General Dynamics, has looked at how this might be done to the F-15 and F-16.

Today's fighters cannot be modified into Stealth aircraft, as the term is applied to the ATF, although some RCS reductions in limited aspects can be achieved. New, lighter airframe materials are usually not worth the cost unless they are applied to the part of the aircraft which is being redesigned anyway.

The Red Team upgrades were based instead on using the ATF engines and avionics. It is relatively easy to fit the F-15 and F-16 with the ATF engines, because they are fairly close in external size, weight and airflow to the F100 and F110. The new avionics are more compact and lighter than current systems, so it is possible to integrate them into existing aircraft designs with some changes to the cooling systems and power supplies. But it is not quite that simple.

"Airplanes are like people," Ben Rich of Lockheed Skunk Works fame has commented. "They all gain weight and they never have enough tail." The beauty of this observation is its truth. Both the F-15 and F-16 have gained weight since they entered service, as more features have been built in. The F100 and F110 engines have been uprated to offset the weight increase, but it is more difficult and expensive to change the wing area, the size of the tail or the internal fuel volume. External fuel tanks have been added to maintain the range, but the higher wing loading and greater inertia take their toll of maneuverability.

It is therefore hardly surprising that the designs produced in the Red Team study, identified as the Falcon 21 and the F-15XX, both came out with new and larger wings. The Falcon 21 was a tailless delta and the F-15XX had a higher-aspect-ratio, thin-section wing made from advanced composite materials, with leading-edge flaps.

Such radical changes cost money. While FSD would cost less than developing the ATF (subsystems could remain common to the older aircraft, and modified F-15s or F-16s could be used for much of the flight-test program), the price tag would be substantial. Performance would be well below that of the ATF, particularly in the supersonic regime.

For the F-15XX, many of the life-cycle-cost drivers (such as engine maintenance and fuel) would be the same as those on the ATF. The Falcon 21, though, would be less expensive to operate than the ATF, and is fairly close in performance to another proposed alternative: a modern "lightweight" fighter with a single F119 or F120, related to the ATF as the F-16 is related to the F-15.

"ATF Lite" would (according to its advocates) be less costly to acquire and to operate than the ATF, could replace both the F-15 and the F-16 (increasing the total production run and reducing overall unit costs) and might be extremely attractive on the export market.

The ATF Lite could match the ATF in almost everything except Stealth and range. To save weight, it would probably have to carry its missiles conformally rather than internally, ruling out Stealth to the degree achieved on ATF. Its head-on RCS could probably be kept quite low, which might be adequate if no power ever establishes the equivalent of the Eastern European SAM belt.

Range is a more difficult problem. ATF Lite is a little smaller than the Eurofighter EFA, which has about half the range of the ATF. A 400 mile operational radius is fine for Europe's Central Region, but a war in that area appears increasingly unlikely. Superimposed on the Middle East, a 400 mile radius begins to look inadequate.

The snag is that the ATF Lite represents half the aircraft for considerably more than half the money. The development cost would be marginally reduced. Removing one engine saves less than ten percent of the flyaway cost. The avionics cost about the same as they do on ATF unless some important capabilities, such as INEWS, are removed completely. The structure cost might be reduced, though certainly not by half, and many items, such as life-support systems and the cockpit, are the same price whether the fighter has one engine or two. Life-cycle cost savings from having a smaller aircraft are real, but are partly offset by the fact that single-engine fighters have a higher accident rate.

Another option facing Pentagon planners is to skip a generation in fighter development, relying on an upgrade such as the F-15XX while proceeding with technology for a new fighter to become operational after 2005; starting, in effect, where the ATF program was in 1982. The keystone of such a trans-century fighter would be a program known as IHPTET (Integrated High-Performance Turbine Engine Technology).

IHPTET is a Pentagon-wide program which aims to improve the key performance numbers of turbine engines by 100 percent by the end of the 1990s. In the case of fighter engines, this means a thrust/weight ratio of 20:1. This makes short take-off and vertical landing (STOVL) possible, with virtually no penalty in weight or in up-and-away performance, and would also increase the fighter's efficiency and range. With an IHPTET-based variable-cycle engine, a fighter the size of ATF Lite might be able to equal the ATF's range. It could replace not only the F-15 and F-16, but the current (or upgraded) versions of the F-14 and F-18 as well.

Such a program may be attractive in theory, but it relies entirely on technology which is in its early stages of development. Historically, it has proven difficult and expensive to develop a new stage in technology without practical, operational experience of the stage before it.

One might also ask who will be around to develop the trans-century fighter when the nation needs it. Industry's investment in ATF has already surpassed $1.5 billion. Not one penny will be recovered if the program is canceled, and no company will ever enter into such a deal again. The entire program will have to be funded by Congress; and, if anyone believes that Congress can be relied upon to make good on a deal over a period of fifteen years . . . well, the line for mouse ears is over there.

Compared with real options, rather than the vague concepts which sometimes catch hold in the lawmakers' minds, ATF/NATF begins to look competitive. It has enough range to operate in any theater. In threat environments less dense than Central Europe, Stealth is still useful, because the ATF can survive with less help from airborne jammers and defense-suppression aircraft, and it is therefore quicker and less costly to maintain and to deploy a credible force.

The stress on low maintenance and reliability, expressed through the way the program has been run as well as through the design of the aircraft, will make even a small ATF force able to generate a large number of sorties. ATF was designed to have a smaller logistics tail, with the Middle East, not Central Europe, in mind. ATF was designed to fight and win against superior odds in Central Europe; but that means a smaller force wields greater weight elsewhere.

If you don't know what wars you may have to fight, ATF may be the best way to fight them.

Appendix

1: ATF data

Dimensions	YF-22	YF-23
Length overall	64 ft 2 in	67 ft 5 in
Wing span	43 ft	43 ft 7 in
Height	17 ft 8.9 in	13 ft 11 in
Wing area	830 sq ft	900 sq ft

Weights (ATF)*

	YF-22	YF-23
Operating empty	31,000 lb	29,000 lb
Internal fuel	22,000 lb	21,000 lb
Normal take-off	58,000 lb	54,000 lb

Performance

Maximum speed,
military power   Mach 1.6, 920 kt

Performance

Maximum speed, maximum power	Mach 2.2, 1,260 kt
Service ceiling	65,000 ft
Take-off or landing field length	3,500 ft
Unrefueled combat radius	750-800 nm

Weights (Navy ATF)

Operating empty	33,000 lb
Internal fuel	25,000 lb
Maximum weapon load	6,000 lb
Normal take-off	65,000 lb

2: ATF, F-15 and EFA data**

Thrust/weight ratio	ATF	F-15C	EFA
Take-off weight, military power	0.9	0.58	0.68
Take-off weight, maximum power	1.34	0.96	1.01
Combat weight, military power	1.17	0.74	0.93
Combat weight, military power	1.75	1.22	1.39

Wing loading	ATF	F-15C	EFA
Take-off weight lb/sq ft	58	81	73
Combat weight lb/sq ft	44	64	53

3: ATF milestones and events

June 1981	First ATF request for information issued
October 1982	ATF defined as 50,000 lb counterair fighter
May 1983	RFP issued for ATF engine development
September 1983	Pratt & Whitney, General Electric selected to build ATF engines
December 1984	USAF Headquarters approves ATF Statement of Operational Need
September 1985	Dem/Val RFP issued
March 1986	Navy agrees to study ATF as F-14D follow-up
April 1986	Deadline for response to Dem/Val RFP
May 1986	Plan to fly ATF prototypes announced
Summer 1986	ATF industrial teams formed
October 1986	Lockheed and Northrop announced as winners
Late 1987	Thrust reversal deleted
Early 1990	Source selection postponed from December 1990
August 1990	First flight of YF-23
September 1990	First flight of YF-22
November 1990	Full-scale development RFP issued

April 1991	ATF and engine winners selected
June 1991	Decision to proceed with FSD and Navy ATF Dem/Val II
Late 1993	Decision to proceed with FSD on Navy ATF
June 1994	ATF first flight
FY1996	Low-rate initial production (LRIP) decision on ATF
January 1997	Navy ATF first flight
FY1998	High-rate ATF production decision
FY1999	ATF initial operation capacity
FY2000	Navy LRIP decision
FY2001	ATF attains peak production rate (48/year)
FY2004	Navy ATF attains peak production rate (36/year)

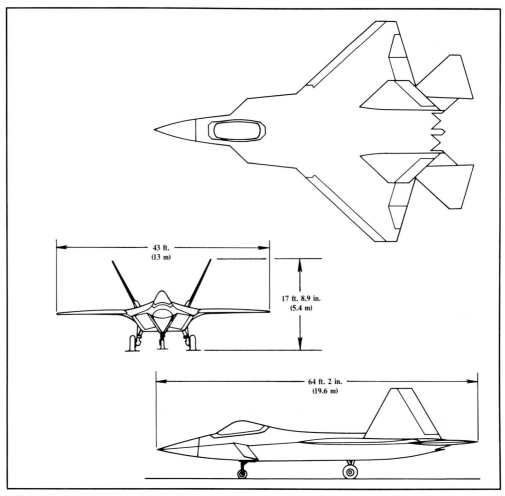

YF–22. Lockheed

4: ATF team members

	YF-22	YF-23
Leader	Lockheed	Northrop
Associates	Boeing	McDonnell Douglas
	General Dynamics	
Engine	General Electric vs Pratt & Whitney	General Electric vs. Pratt & Whitney
Radar array	Westinghouse/Texas Instruments	Texas Instruments/Westinghouse
IRST	General Electric/Martin Marietta	Martin Marietta/General Electric
FCS	GEC Astronics	General Electric
Navigation	TRW (ICNIA)	TRW (ICNIA)
EW/ESM	Sanders/General Electric	ITT/Westinghouse
Computer modules	Texas Instruments	Unisys
Signal processors	Hughes	AT&T

*PAVs only. Lockheed FSD configuration is likely to be lighter. All data estimated except for dimensions.
**Take-off weight with full missile load and full internal fuel; F-15C with 600 gal external tank, EFA with two 300 gal external tanks. Combat weight with part internal fuel and full weapon load.

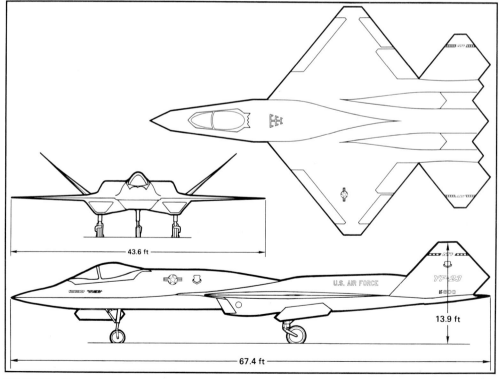

YF-23. Northrop

Index